Jan Luba is a barrister who has specialized in social security and housing law. He has worked in the Citizens Advice Bureau service, with law centres and as legal officer to the Child Poverty Action Group. He is the author of a number of books and articles on housing and social welfare law and is presently Chair of the Legal Action Group.

GW00418421

Other titles in the *Sphere Rights Guides* series:

Forthcoming:

SPHERE RIGHTS GUIDES
Series Editor: Andrew Arden

THE OWNER-OCCUPIER HANDBOOK

JAN LUBA

SPHERE REFERENCE

A SPHERE BOOK

First published in Great Britain
by Sphere Books Ltd 1990

Copyright © Jan Luba 1990

Typeset in Plantin by Leaper & Gard Ltd, Bristol, England
Printed and bound in Great Britain by
The Guernsey Press

ISBN 0-7474-0219-0

Sphere Books Ltd
A Division of
Macdonald & Co (Publishers) Ltd
27 Wrights Lane, London W8 5TZ
A member of Maxwell Pergamon Publishing Corporation plc

Contents

3. Your Home and Your Family

What rights have members of my family got to live in my
home?

4. Repairs and Improvements to Your Home   59

5. Letting Your Home or Parts of Your Home   73

Contents

6. Your Home and Your Neighbours   86

How would I go about getting a council house or flat when I leave my present home?

How do I go about getting a place in a retirement, residential care or nursing home when I sell my present home?

What if I am going to lose my present home and cannot arrange another permanent home to move to?

What if I am offered accommodation by my new employer?

Why should I make a complaint?

What is the best way to make a complaint?
> *Solicitors*
> *Surveyors*
> *Valuers*
> *Estate Agents*
> *Building Societies*
> *Builders*
> *Insurance Companies*
> *Contractors*
> *Local Councils*
> *Government Departments*

Where can I get general advice?

What about specialist advice on housing?

How do I go about getting legal advice?

What is legal aid?

Introduction

This book is written for homeowners – that is, people who currently own (rather than rent) their house or flat. Most householders in Britain now own their own home. If you are a homeowner your property is perhaps your most valuable personal asset. Not only is it your own home and perhaps your family's home but it probably represents most of your capital wealth. For those reasons you will want to get the best from it and make sure that you don't lose it.

This handbook sets out to be a basic guide to the most important rights and obligations that homeowners have in Britain today. It covers a very broad range from the basics of owning your present home to the process of finding a new one. But precisely because homes are so important you should bear in mind that this book is not a detailed or exhaustive explanation of the law or your legal rights. If you want to resolve a particular problem or issue which concerns your home, I hope you find some guidance in these pages. But for the definitive or conclusive position you ought to take specialist advice – whether from a lawyer or other adviser. Wherever possible the book will direct you to a specialist source of further advice or information.

The last chapter, Making Complaints and Taking Advice, helps you to make the link between the issues discussed in the book and the places giving advice. You could take this book with you so that you can draw the adviser's attention to the point you are particularly interested in.

In any book of this size there is inevitably a need to concentrate on the most fundamental aspects of the subject and as a result some material which may be of less importance is not included. Most time and space is devoted to the issues of most direct concern to the home-owner on a modest or mid-range income. But areas of interest to all types of homeowner – for example relations with neighbours – are dealt with too.

This book is one of a series containing help and advice about basic legal rights relating to property and your attention is directed to companion volumes which may be of relevance, particularly the *Mobile Homes Handbook* and, where the advice in this volume needs to be supplemented, to *The Private Tenants, Public Tenants,* and *Homeless Persons Handbooks.*

The legal position relating to property rights is constantly changing. New court cases are decided all the time and new laws are constantly being passed by Parliament. This book was written in the Spring of 1989 when substantial parts of property law were under review (particularly in relation to house renovation grants and homelessness). I have only attempted an outline of the legal position relating to property in England and Wales. Scotland has its own and rather different laws about property and land ownership. There is one theme that dominates the whole book. It is that a problem is better resolved sooner rather than later. Each year very many homeowners lose their rights and in some cases their entire homes due to a failure to act swiftly in the face of difficulties. There is never a better time to check out any question that's concerning you than right now! This book is designed to help you find the answer or solution most appropriate to your own personal circumstances.

1: Owning Your Home

What are the different ways in which a home may be owned?

There are many ways in which property in Britain can be owned. The form of ownership most immediately associated with possession of residential property is *freehold* ownership and both houses and (less commonly) flats may be owned freehold. But many homeowners have their homes on a lease for a fixed period (sometimes as long as 999 years) which gives them *leasehold* ownership. Both houses and flats can be owned leasehold. In this chapter I explain the differences between leasehold and freehold, the circumstances in which leasehold can be converted into freehold and the effects of those different forms of ownership.

There are differences between the legal ownership of property and other forms of ownership. There are also important differences in the situations that arise if property is owned by one person alone or by several people together or by individuals in common with an organization. These are also dealt with in this chapter.

What does owning the freehold mean?

The word *freehold* has its origins in the ancient ownership of land in Britain by the monarchy and feudal lords. Most ordinary people 'held' their land in return for some sort of commitment to their overlord. As the ancient order was removed and replaced, the best form of ownership came to be *freehold*, that is, land held free of any commitment to a superior owner.

Today it is the essence of freehold ownership that the owner is free to hold the property indefinitely in his or her

own name and to dispose of it as he or she wishes. The
legal name for this sort of ownership is 'the fee simple
absolute in possession' and you will find this sort of word-
ing in the documentation you had when you bought your
home.

If you own the freehold, it gives you the ownership not
only of the land itself (within its boundaries) but also of
any buildings on it, the earth below it and everything
above it.

Your right to the freehold (sometimes called your 'title'
of ownership) will be set out in a legal document called a
deed – hence the phrase 'title-deeds'. Because this document is the authority for your ownership of the freehold it
is vital for any transactions you might want to enter into,
such as the sale or disposal of your property. It is for this
reason that lenders advancing money to people buying
freehold property require the deeds to be deposited with
them until the loan is repaid.

What does owning a home leasehold mean?

Being the *leasehold* owner means that instead of having
the freehold ownership of the property the homeowner
has leased the accommodation which comprises the
home. A lease is an agreement whereby the freehold
owner of land (in the first instance) confers a right for
some other person to have the land for a fixed period. At
the end of the fixed period the ownership reverts back to
the freeholder. We usually speak of people who have their
homes on a lease originally granted for a longer period
than 21 years as homeowners (the position of people with
shorter leases is dealt with in *The Private Tenants Handbook* in this series) and some leases are very long indeed –
999 years is the normal maximum.

Often the person granted the lease by the freeholder
may themselves grant a shorter lease to another person.
So you could start with a 99 year lease from A (free-

holder) to B (leaseholder). Then B could grant a lease for, say, 49 years to C who also then becomes a leaseholder. This further type of lease is properly called an 'under-lease' because it comes under the original lease. Because there can sometimes be quite a long chain of underleases from the original freeholder, the homeowner's own lease may not necessarily be the one from the freeholder. In the rest of this chapter (and throughout this book) I use the term 'lessor' to mean the person from whom the home-owner has his or her lease whether that person is the free-holder or another leaseholder.

All the details about your ownership of your home will be set out in the lease itself. This will say whether the lease is granted by the freeholder or whether it is one in a series of underleases. The various clauses of the lease will explain respectively the obligations of the lessor and your-self for things like repairs, insurance, etc., as well as set-ting out precisely what property you have acquired under the lease.

The obligations that the clauses of the lease impose on you are very important. If you fail to observe them, your lessor can take steps to bring your lease to an early end (this is called 'forfeiture'). Should your lessor take any steps to try to do that, take advice immediately (see page 130). If you act promptly you will have the right to apply for 'relief from forfeiture' if the case comes to court – which will mean your keeping your home. By that stage you will probably have taken legal advice (see page 131). For the situation of a homeowner whose lease is about to expire or has expired see page 15.

Can I change my home from leasehold to freehold?

The obvious way to change from leasehold to freehold is to see if the freehold owner will sell you his freehold interest in your home. If he is not prepared to sell to you voluntarily, you may have the legal right to buy the freehold. The way in which you can use this right is different according to whether your home is a house or flat. But before you consider using a legal right to buy the freehold it is still worth inquiring what price the freeholder would ask for a voluntary sale. If you are quoted a price don't just accept it at face value. Ask a valuer (see below) to estimate what the purchase price would be if you were to exercise your legal right to buy the freehold. If, rather unusually, the freeholder is offering a better price than you would get in exercising your legal rights, then you should consider proceeding with a voluntary sale.

The legal right to buy the freehold of a *house* has been available to leasehold owners since 1967. You can exercise this right (sometimes called 'enfranchising') if you can satisfy all the following conditions:

(a) You occupy the house as your only or main home.

(b) You hold a lease which was originally granted for a period of more than 21 years and is for the whole house.

(c) You have occupied the house as your home for the last three years (or for three of the last ten years).

(d) Your lease is for a low rent (there is a formula for working this out but it covers most ordinary houses).

(e) The house is within certain rateable value limits (again there is a formula for working this out, which covers most ordinary houses).

If you have inherited the lease from a member of your family you can, for the purpose of calculating the three-year qualifying period in (c), add to your own period of occupation the period that family member spent in occupation.

You still have the right to the freehold even if you have tenants in the house with you (see Chapter 5) or you jointly own (see page 12) the lease with another person. If there is a series of leases of which yours is the last one, you will have to buy out the lessors of the other leases as part of buying the freehold but the total cost should not be more than you would have had to pay to the freeholder normally.

You start the process by serving a formal notice on your freeholder (and also on any other leaseholders in a chain of leases above yours). If your right to buy is accepted by the freeholder you then negotiate a price. (If your freeholder refuses to accept your right to buy, other than for one of the very narrow range of reasons allowed, you could go to court to enforce it.) If you can't agree a price, it can be fixed by the independent Leasehold Valuation Tribunal (with a right of appeal to the Lands Tribunal (see page 91).) If you can't afford the fixed price you can withdraw at that point.

If you are thinking about buying the freehold of your house there are several things to consider. First, take advantage of the free advice available – there is an excellent free Government booklet called *Leasehold Reform: A Guide for Leaseholders and Landlords* (Housing Booklet No.9), which you can get from a Citizens' Advice Bureau or local advice centre. Next, consider the fees and expenses you will have to incur – you have to pay not only your own costs but those of the freeholder too. Try to get some firm estimates from solicitors in advance as to what your own costs would be (see page 114). Then, obviously, there is the question of the price of the freehold itself. You will need to get some advice about the appropriate price to pay and may need a surveyor or valuer to assist you. There is more information about surveyors and valuers on page 115.

Generally speaking, it is a good idea to buy the freehold of your home if you can. The earlier in the lease you exercise the right to buy the lower the price is likely to be. (See pages 15–6 for what will happen if the lease is about to expire and you do not buy.)

How do I go about buying the freehold of my flat?

If your home is a flat and your lessor is not willing to sell his or her interest or the freehold to you voluntarily, you don't have the same right to buy the freehold as that available to certain leaseholders of houses. But if the lessor under your lease (who might be the freeholder) proposes to sell, you might have a legal right to first consideration as buyer. This is called the *Right of First Refusal* and became law in 1987. You qualify for the Right of First Refusal if you can meet all the following conditions:

(a) You have the lease of a flat.

(b) You do not own more than one other flat in the building.

(c) More than half the flats in the building are held by other tenants or leaseholders.

(d) Your flat is owned for private not business purposes.

If you qualify and your lessor intends to sell, he or she must give notice offering you the opportunity to buy and stating the proposed terms and the price. You will probably not be the only leaseholder in the building to get such a notice. If you are interested in the possibility of buying, you should make contact with the leaseholders of the other flats because if you are going to buy you must get the support of more than 50% of the notified lease-holders in order to move forward.

If there is support, the next thing to consider is financing the purchase. If you have not already taken advice, this will be the stage at which to do so. You will have to work out how the money will be raised, how the purchase will be organized, who will buy (will it be some individuals on behalf of others or will a company need to be formed to act for all the purchasers?) and how the property will be managed after the purchase has gone through.

If you are thinking of exercising these rights you need

to act promptly because the lessor's notice may only be effective for the minimum two month period. Get a copy of the free leaflet *Right of First Refusal* (Housing Booklet No.28) from your local Citizens' Advice Bureau or other advice centre. Also, write to the Incorporated Society of Valuers & Auctioneers (address on page 128) for their free leaflet *Offered the freehold – should I buy?* For a comprehensive but reasonably priced guide see *Owning Your Flat* from SHAC (see page 131). If, after having considered this information, you decide to move ahead, try to get your local Private Residents' Association involved – the address of the National Federation of Residents' Associations (which can give you the contact address for any local group) is 11 Dartmouth St, London SW1H 9BL. This may provide a good way of organizing matters such as sharing the costs of lawyers and valuers with other leaseholders.

If your lessor ignores your right of first refusal and sells the property to someone else, you have the power to force that buyer to sell to you as long as you can serve notice on them within two months of their telling you that they are the new owners. They may then have to sell to you at no more than the price they paid. If you are in this sort of situation follow the steps I suggested in the last paragraph.

My home is owned leasehold, how can I be sure who the freeholder is?

Your immediate lessor must give you a *contact* address in England or Wales and if you ask the person managing your property, he or she must give you the *actual* name and address of the lessor if you put your request in writing. Any demand for rent or service charges must also show your lessor's name and address. If this information is not provided, you can withhold payment of the service charge demanded until it is provided (although for the ground rent see page 42). If your lessor sells the property to someone else the new owner must write to you within two months of purchase letting you know that they have bought and giving their name and address.

If you are not receiving this sort of information, get a copy of the appropriate free leaflet from your local advice centre and then consider taking advice about enforcing your legal rights (see page 131). If your home is a house, the leaflet to ask for is *The Rights & Duties of Landlords and Tenants of Houses* (Housing Booklet No.26). If your home is a flat ask for *The Management of Flats – the Rights & Duties of Landlord & Tenant* (Housing Booklet No.27).

An alternative would be to search the official records of the property for the name and address of the owner. You can do this by contacting the local District Office of the Land Registry (see page 14). Ask them to send you Form 108 and an explanatory booklet. If you complete and return the form, the Registry should be able to give you the owner's name and address.

Can I change my home from freehold to leasehold?

Although this is a rather unusual thing to want to do, it certainly can be done. It will involve you selling or trans-ferring your freehold to someone else on the basis that they will then grant you a lease of the property. For obvi-ous reasons the procedure is called 'sale and lease-back'. You might want to do this in order to obtain a lump sum for your home by selling the freehold yet want to continue to live there in return for making regular payments. However, because the procedure involves such an import-ant matter as losing the freehold of your home it needs to be approached with care. Take independent legal advice (see page 131). Certainly, do not just rely on assurances given to you by the person suggesting you pursue this sort of transaction.

What if my home is a freehold flat?

The idea of holding property as a freehold owner (that is with the indefinite right to the space above and below the surface of the land) does not easily square with ownership of flats. However there are now some flats owned freehold, usually those created by conversion of large old houses. The title deeds will describe exactly what parts of the building each freeholder owns and will probably all contain similar binding promises (called positive covenants – see page 89) by which each owner pledges rights of support and access, etc. to the others. This works perfectly well until one of the freeholders dies or sells his property. Because the positive covenants only normally bind the first freeholder there can be practical problems about enforcing obligations, on which all the freeholders will inter-depend, on newcomers. The only way to avoid these difficulties is to get the newcomers to enter into the same commitments as their predecessors.

It is very sensible to take advice before buying a flat freehold and because of the legal and practical difficulties it will prove harder to find a mortgage for a freehold flat than a leasehold one.

Is the legal owner always the real owner of a property?

The legal owner is the person whose name is shown on the title deeds of a freehold property or on the lease where the property is owned leasehold. If there is more than one named person, then the people whose names are shown are joint legal owners (see below).

It is quite possible that the true owner is not the legal owner of the property at all. For example, this might be because the true owner is under eighteen. An adult therefore has to take the legal ownership on behalf of the child. Similarly, the true owner may not want to be identified on the legal records so a nominee becomes the legal owner on his or her behalf.

11

Alternatively, the purchase of the property might be contributed to by several joint buyers who agree that only one of them should be legal owner and hold the property on behalf of the others.

In all these instances and in other similar cases the true owners of the property are the people for whose benefit the legal owner holds the property. The law calls these people the 'beneficial' owners. The legal owner holds the property on trust for the beneficial owner. What this means in practice is that the legal owner must not do anything to prejudice the interests of the beneficial owner. When the property is sold the proceeds belong to the beneficial owner rather than the legal owner.

What is joint ownership?

Joint legal ownership occurs when the ownership of property passes to more than one person in a deed or lease. There is a variety of ways in which you can acquire a home jointly with other people and these are described in full in *Buying Your Home with Other People* (from Shelter – address on page 131). If the home has been purchased in the names of individuals there are two ways in which the home might be jointly owned – as true joint owners or as owners in shares.

In a true joint ownership, all the named people together own the whole property. Therefore, if one of the joint owners dies the whole property remains with the surviving joint owners. When there is only one surviving joint owner that person becomes the sole owner of the whole.

The other form of joint ownership is ownership in shares. Each individual has a share or stake in the home. Perhaps each has an equal share (the home is owned 50/50) or there are different shares (for example, one owns 30% the other 70%). In this type of joint ownership, the ownership of the property does not pass to the surviving joint owner when the other dies. Instead, the deceased's share in the property passes into his or her Estate to be distributed under his or her will.

It is possible to change from the first to the second type of joint ownership by one joint owner serving a notice on the others. If you want to do this, take legal advice (see page 131).

For the difficulties which can arise from disagreements between joint owners, see pages 50–1. For the position where the joint owner is your spouse see pages 51–2.

If your documents show that your home was purchased with someone else and you are described as 'joint beneficial owners' this means that, irrespective of your relative contributions to the purchase price and other costs, you own the property equally.

What is shared ownership?

Shared ownership is the name given to an arrangement under which you buy your home in stages. While you are buying it you part-own it with the person selling. You start off by buying a proportion of the value of your home by taking out a long lease. The rest of your home remains owned by the freeholder and you pay the freeholder rent for that proportion. The legal scheme worked out between you and the freeholder gives you the right to buy further proportions of the house or flat until you own it all.

The majority of owners interested in making property available for shared ownership are local councils, other public bodies and housing associations.

If you are in a shared ownership arrangement, your rights and responsibilities will largely be regulated by the terms of your lease. Also you may have taken out a mortgage in order to finance part of the purchase price so you will need to observe any conditions which that imposes. Under the arrangements you will probably have the right to buy further proportions of the property at any time. When you have bought it all you will have the right to the freehold if your home is a house. If your home is a flat you will be entitled to a long lease at a nominal rent. The special position of shared-ownership homeowners is described in the free leaflets *Local Authority Shared Ownership* (Housing Booklet No.15) available from Citizens' Advice Bureaux and other advice centres, and *Shared Ownership* from the Housing Corporation, 149 Tottenham Court Rd, London W1P 0BN.

Are there any official records of ownership?
Yes. In stages, all the country's land is being recorded, mapped and registered with the *Land Registry* which has several District Offices covering different parts of the country. The plan is that eventually every plot of land will have a record in the official register at the Land Registry. Each will be given a number and a record will be kept of the legal ownership of the land and any changes of ownership.

This registration of the ownership of land is being gradually expanded to cover all areas. Those buying or selling homes in areas of registered land must notify the Land Registry each time the legal ownership of the land changes. The register also records other useful information concerning the land such as rights of way (see page 91), etc.

For those parts of the country where the land has not yet been registered another set of official records is kept called the *Land Charges Register*. This allows details to be recorded of the interests that people have in specific property – for example it allows details of a mortgage to be included against the description of a specific property. The Register enables a prospective purchaser to see what interests other people may have recorded against a property in addition to those of the person selling.

Can a person become an owner through 'squatters' rights'?

Yes. The colloquial phrase 'squatters' rights' refers to a legal rule called *adverse possession*. This rule says that if a person occupies land for more than 12 years and is not within that time challenged or displaced by the owner, the 'squatter' himself takes over the ownership from the true owner. If the original owner was a freeholder, the 'squatter' gets the freehold. If the original owner was a leaseholder, the 'squatter' becomes the owner for the remainder of the lease.

The basis of the rule is that an owner has a legal right to take action to get possession back from a trespasser but that this right cannot be enforced after 12 years from the first date of unlawful occupation. In order to claim the benefit of this rule squatters must be able to show that they have openly occupied or taken possession of the property without the owner's consent and used it as their own (this is easily demonstrated if fences have been put around – or buildings erected upon – the land). They must not have paid money to or in any way recognized the rights of the true owner.

If you want to assert that you have become the owner of your home on this basis you should take legal advice (see page 131) because there are lots of exceptions to the normal rule and difficulties can arise with the operation of the role in practice. If, as is more likely, you want to claim squatters' rights over some property on the boundaries of your home see pages 86–7.

I own my home on a lease, what will happen when the lease expires?

Obviously, because the lease will have ended this will seriously affect your rights to your home. If you own a *house* on a lease it is well worth considering buying the freehold as early as possible in your lease to avoid this happening (see page 5). If you can't afford (or don't wish) to buy the freehold of the house you can apply for an extension of your current lease for a further 50 years beyond its original duration if you meet the qualifying conditions described on page 6.

If your home is a *flat* you may have the Right of First Refusal in relation to the freehold (see page 8) but this does not help if your lessor is not proposing to sell even if he is prepared to negotiate a new lease with you.

However, just because your lease expires this does not mean you can be immediately evicted from your home whether it is a house or a flat. Your lease will be treated as running on. Even if the lessor serves a notice to end it, you will then have the status of a *protected tenant* with an indefinite right to remain in occupation. Your rights are described in DoE Fourth Edition, October 1973. Because this puts you in a rather strong negotiating position the most common outcome of this situation is that the lessor offers a fresh lease (usually for a minimum of 21 years).

At the time this book was being written, Parliament was considering changes to the rules about expired leases which would water-down the rights of lessees once the lease expired. For leases granted after the date the Local Government and Housing Act 1989 takes effect, new rules apply when they expire. Leases granted before that date will not be affected unless their expiry falls after 15 January 1999.

Under the proposed new regime, the homeowner with an expired lease becomes an *assured private tenant* which means they can be charged a higher rent than would have been the case before and there is reduced security of tenure. If the expiry of your lease will be covered by the new regime, it is worth taking advice now about what your position will be (see page 130).

What is 'ownership by rental purchase'?

Rental purchase is an arrangement under which you buy your home in instalments. You move in under the terms of an agreement to eventually buy and you make regular payments to the owner. The agreement usually provides that when you make the last of the payments the ownership of the property transfers to you. Until that date you are not the owner of your home.

In the recent past, rental purchase agreement have been used in cases where people did not really want to buy but would have preferred to rent. Some landlords offered accommodation on the rental purchase basis to avoid the Rent Acts. If you never really intended to buy when you took on a rental purchase agreement, it is worth taking legal advice now (see page 131). You may be able to get the agreement declared a tenancy by a court (which would give you security of tenure) or, alternatively, it might be that if you stay with the present agreement you could buy at less than market price.

If you have a genuine rental purchase agreement, despite the fact that you do not become the owner until the last payment, you do have some legal rights to stay in your home even if you can no longer afford the full payments or you and the true owner are in dispute (see Losing Your Home, chapter 7).

2: Paying For Your Home

What sorts of payments do I have to make on my home?

If you are still buying your home, probably the most important payments you will make will be those which repay your loan or *mortgage*. But this will usually be only one of a series of regular payments you may have to make on your home. You will probably pay an amount every year for *buildings insurance* to cover you against damage to your home. Then there will be *contents insurance* to provide protection against loss or damage to the personal possessions in your home. You might also have a separate *mortgage protection* insurance policy to cover you in case you can no longer repay your mortgage. Until April 1990 you will also have been liable for *general rates* on the property you occupy as your home. Finally, if you are a leaseholder you might be required to make regular payments under your lease either for *ground rent* or *service charges* or other specified payments.

In this chapter I look at all these types of payments and consider what limits there are to what can be charged, how you could get financial help with the payments and what to do if you are in difficulty with your payments. Obviously most owner-occupiers will also have to make payments for gas, electricity, water and other services and advice on those sorts of payments is available in the *Money Advice Handbook* in this series. If you are concerned about payments to do with the costs of repairs and improvements, see chapter 4 (Repairs and Improvements to Your Home).

What is a mortgage?

A mortgage is the security or guarantee a lender has that you will repay money loaned to you to buy your home. It is a powerful guarantee because if the loan is not repaid it allows the lender to enforce the loan by ultimately re-possessing the property and selling it to raise enough money to repay the debt. The mortgage terms will be set out in a document that was drawn up by your lender and your solicitor at the time you bought your home. The mortgage is recorded against the official records of the property itself (see page 14) in order to prevent you selling to someone else without repaying your lender.

In the official jargon the person borrowing the money is called a *mortgagor* and the organization doing the lending is called the *mortgagee*. In this chapter I use the words 'lender' and 'borrower' in place of these terms.

What are the different types of mortgage?

There are a whole range of different types of mortgage and you need to be clear which type you have because this affects the way you make repayments and the help that might be available to you in clearing your debt. The most common types of mortgage are:

1. Capital repayment mortgage

A capital repayment mortgage requires that you repay the loan over a fixed period (usually 20 or 25 years) by regular instalments which are usually payable monthly. Each payment is first put towards clearing the interest due on the loan and then the capital. Over the years the amount of interest is reduced and more and more capital is repaid. At the end of the fixed period the whole debt is cleared. This type of arrangement is sometimes called an *annuity mortgage*. If it were not for the fact that the lender usually has power to change the rate of interest during the period of the loan, your repayments would be the same every month through the whole of your mortgage. As it is, because interest rates change periodically, your monthly repayments will go up and down accordingly.

Some lenders offer a variant of the capital repayment mortgage, under which payments in the first few years are collected at a lower rate but increase later. These arrangements are based on the proposition that your income will grow over the period of the mortgage so that you pay less at the outset but more later. You should only take one of these loans if you are sure that your income will in fact increase over the years (in many households the income falls after the first few years when one partner gives up work to care for children).

2. Endowment mortgage

An endowment mortgage is rather different. You make regular (usually monthly) payments over a fixed period of years. These payments will rise or fall from time to time as your lender has power to adjust the rates of interest. But your payments only clear the interest on the loan not the capital itself. This falls due for repayment as a lump sum at the end of the mortgage term. In order to ensure that you will have the money to pay that capital sum, your lender requires you to take out an endowment policy with a life assurance company. Under the policy you make regular monthly premium payments (often collected by your lender together with the interest payments) and these guarantee that at the end of the mortgage period the assurance company will clear the capital debt. If you die before the end of the mortgage period the assurance company will clear the balance outstanding on the mortgage.

There are two main types of endowment mortgage and the papers you are given when you take out the loan should tell you which one you have: a 'guaranteed' or 'non-profit' endowment plan is the simplest type – the assurance company simply clears the capital lump sum; a 'with profits' endowment plan will not only cover the capital sum but will promise an extra amount at the end of the term (this might be called a profit, bonus or dividend) but you will be paying slightly higher premiums.

There are other types of mortgage which work on the endowment method but which invest your premiums slightly differently and may be called 'unit-linked' or 'investment-related', etc., according to the method used.

3. 'Low cost', 'low start' or 'build up' mortgage

This is usually a variant of the 'with profits' endowment mortgage described above. Under this sort of arrangement you make monthly payments of interest and life assurance premiums but the life assurance company guarantees a sum lower than your total loan, e.g. £20,000 instead of £30,000. The idea is that by the time you come to repay the capital at the end of the term, the balance can be made good by 'profits' earned from investing your insurance premiums. If you die before the end of the mortgage term, the assurance company pays the whole capital debt.

4. Pension mortgage

A pension mortgage is different again. This also involves you borrowing a lump sum to buy your home and making interest-only monthly payments. The capital is repaid as a lump sum when you reach pension age by a pension plan into which you have been making private pension payments. If you have this type of arrangement, it was probably taken out when you were self-employed or did not belong to a company pension scheme and may have very considerable tax advantages. Your lender gets a guarantee of repayment because the pension company will usually arrange with you that it will pay off the capital part of the loan direct to the lender before paying any pension to you.

What is a 'second' mortgage?

In ordinary language this would probably be the mortgage you took out when you bought a second home! What it in fact means is a further loan, again guaranteed by a mortgage, but secured against the value of your present home. The purpose of the loan would not usually have been to buy the home (that was what the 'first' mortgage was for). Most commonly the loan will be to finance repairs or improvements or to meet other debts or expenses.

Because the lender for your second mortgage is further down the pecking-order of your creditors than the first lender, you will usually be charged a higher rate of interest and loaned a smaller amount over a shorter period than would be the case with a first mortgage.

This type of arrangement is often called a 'secured loan' because you are pledging the value of your home (or part of its value) as security for the loan.

What is a 'remortgage'?

A 'remortgage' simply means taking out a new fresh mortgage which clears your existing mortgages and takes their place. You might remortgage your property from choice (where taking out one fresh mortgage would be cheaper than carrying on with several current ones) or from necessity (for example, where your mortgage was arranged through your former employer and cannot be continued now you are no longer in that employment).

Remortgages can be advantageous because you may find that a responsible lender is willing to lend you a large sum at a reasonable rate of interest to clear off several existing high-interest-rate mortgages. This is called 'redeeming' the earlier mortgages. There is more about this in the section entitled How can I reduce my mortgage repayments (page 25).

What will happen to my mortgage if I die before it is paid off?

The lender with whom you took out your first mortgage will probably have suggested that you paid into an insurance policy to cover this eventuality.

For a *capital repayment mortgage* (see page 19) a separate mortgage protection policy can be cheaply arranged. This will guarantee to clear whatever amount of your mortgage is still outstanding when you die. The premium you pay will depend on your age at the date you enter into the policy. You don't have to take a policy arranged through your lender and indeed any life policy you presently have may provide this sort of cover already. This sort of protection will ensure that any family dependent upon you are not faced with the mortgage debt if you die.

An alternative is a *term assurance* policy. This is slightly different because it guarantees to pay, on death, not merely whatever amount is left outstanding on the loan but the *whole* amount of the original loan if you die within the term of the original loan. So, if your mortgage was £50,000 and you have paid off £25,000 by the time of your death, the assurance company pays £50,000 which your dependants use to clear the debt and keep the balance.

Whichever type of *endowment mortgage* you have, the life assurance endowment policy will clear the whole capital debt.

If you have a *pension mortgage* you will need a life policy of the type described above or a provision in your pension that, in the event of your death, your family will be paid enough to clear the mortgage.

Am I entitled to tax relief on my mortgage?

Yes. If the mortgage was taken out to buy or improve your only or principal home you can get tax relief on any interest you pay for loans up to a certain amount. At the time of writing the maximum is £30,000. Even if your mortgage is for more than that amount, you qualify for tax relief on the first £30,000. Only one loan qualifies for relief at a time although exceptionally you can get relief on two loans where there is an overlap between your moving into a new home and selling your old one.

Under the *Mortgage Interest Relief at Source* (or MIRAS) scheme the lender works out what your interest repayments would be after allowing tax relief at the basic rate on up to £30,000 worth of your loan. You then pay that net amount to the lender and if you only pay tax at the basic rate your personal income tax code remains unchanged. If you are due more tax relief because you pay tax at higher rates, you claim the balance from the Inland Revenue. You can get more information from the free leaflet *MIRAS* (Booklet No. IR 63), from your local PAYE Tax Enquiry Office (address and telephone number in the phone book under Inland Revenue).

What if I get into difficulties with my mortgage?

A mortgage repayment period is a very long time – possibly as much as 25 or 30 years. Over that sort of period any number of developments might occur which make repayments more difficult to manage. At the simplest, the rates of interest charged might rise so high as to make regular payments more difficult. Alternatively, you might experience problems because of developments in your personal life – loss of employment, sickness or disability, etc.

The golden rule is always the same – act promptly and get good advice! Many people in Britain place their homes in jeopardy every year simply by 'putting off the evil day' and not getting to grips with mortgage problems. Unless you are deliberately neglecting to pay your mortgage, there is very little likelihood of you losing your home if you act promptly and take sensible advice.

Dealing with mortgage payment difficulties is just the same as dealing with any other sort of debt. There are two issues to consider: how to reduce the amount of the regular payments and how to increase income so you can meet the repayments. These are covered below.

How can I reduce my mortgage repayments?

The first thing to consider is whether your loan is from a responsible lending institution like a building society or major bank. Too often, high repayment (first or second) mortgages are arranged with finance companies or other institutions charging excessive rates of interest or seeking high levels of repayment. If this might be your situation make inquiries with one of the major lending institutions to see whether they might be prepared to clear your existing loan or loans and start you on a fresh basis. The process is called remortgaging and is described on page 22. It might mean your taking a larger loan but should mean lower interest rates and a longer repayment period – thereby reducing your monthly bill.

What you do next depends on the type of mortgage you have and how many you have. In the pages that follow I set out some basic guidelines. If you are on a low income you might find it helpful to get the free leaflet *Assistance with Mortgage Payments* from the Building Societies Association (address on page 128) or see the latest edition of the *Rights Guide for Home Owners* published by SHAC (address on page 131).

If you just have one *capital repayment mortgage* there are two ways in which your lender might reduce your monthly repayments. The first is by extending the term over which you must repay your loan, from its present period to a longer one – say from 20 to 25 years. This will reduce the capital element in your monthly payments although the interest collected will stay the same. It means your debt will take longer to clear but there is the immediate prospect of lower payments and the possibility that if circumstances change for the better in the future you could clear the loan ahead of schedule. The second method of reducing your monthly payments is to get your lender to accept 'interest-only payments' and to defer collection of the capital. This can be arranged for a short or longer period. It is particularly useful if you can claim the benefit income support (described on page 29) because that will provide cash help with some or all of the interest payable.

The sooner you approach your lender with an explanation of your difficulties the more likely they are to agree to one or other of these options. From your point of view, the 'interest only' payments option might be preferable because it will lead to an immediate reduction in payments (although only a modest reduction if you have only recently taken on the mortgage) and provide help for the short-term crisis without over-extending the duration of the loan. Make an appointment to see an official at the offices of your lender or write a letter setting out your circumstances and asking for either or both of the options to be considered.

The approach to reducing payments under an *endowment mortgage* is rather different because your regular monthly repayment is made up of two parts – a payment to the life assurance company (the premium) and an interest payment to the lender. The danger of missing payments is that most policies are automatically cancelled if a certain number of payments are missed. You should check your own policy to see what it says about missed payments (most will give a few months' grace). If your difficulties are very short-term this may provide all the breathing space you need. If not, you need seriously to consider the possibility of reducing your regular payments by switching to a capital repayment mortgage (described on page 19). This change will require the involvement of both your lender and the assurance company. Start with your lender to check that a capital repayment mortgage would in fact be cheaper in your case and that the 'administrative charges' for making a switch are not prohibitive. If your lender arranged the original endowment policy, they can then contact the insurers to arrange the necessary terms. If you arranged the policy yourself, you will need to check over it to be sure that you can surrender it and switch to a capital repayment mortgage. Once again the golden rule is to contact the lender and assurance company as soon as possible so that new arrangements can be made before you get seriously into debt.

If you have several mortgages secured on your home, perhaps with different lenders, you may find it very difficult to cover all the repayments and prevent arrears. You should consider whether it is worth while making a fresh start by remortgaging your home (see page 22 for what this means) and taking one completely fresh mortgage from your preferred lender. Find out what outstanding payments you owe to each of your lenders, work out your projected future income and take the information along to a meeting with a responsible lender and see if they can help with a remortgage.

What if my lender refuses to co-operate with me?
If you have made a reasonable proposal for rearranging your affairs to cover mortgage repayments, a responsible lender would usually accept the proposals rather than see arrears accrue and have to consider repossession. If you feel you have been reasonable but the lender's representative you are dealing with is uncooperative, ask to speak to someone higher up in the organization – perhaps at the Regional or Head Office. If you think you are being treated harshly or unfairly, you could make a complaint to an independent Ombudsman who will investigate.

If your lender is a Bank, write to the Banking Ombudsman, Citadel House, 5–11 New Fetter Lane, London EC4A 1BR (01 583 1395). If your lender is a building society, it will have an internal complaints procedure and you should ask for the details. If, having made your complaint in that way, you are not satisfied, write to the Office of the Building Society Ombudsman, 35–37 Grosvenor Gardens, London SW1X 7AW (01 931 0044). If your lender is a local authority, write to the Commission for Local Administration, 21 Queen Anne's Gate, London SW1H 9BU (01 222 5622) and ask for a complaint form and information booklet. If you are having problems with a life assurance company write to the Office of the Insurance Ombudsman at 31 Southampton Row, London WC1B 5HJ.

Can I get any other regular help with paying my mortgage?

First you should check that you are not already paying too much under your mortgage. Make sure you are only making payments net of basic rate tax relief under the MIRAS scheme (explained on page 24). Then look at the section on page 25 which deals with reducing your mortgage repayments to see if any of the options there would apply in your case.

Once you have established that you are paying the right amount and that the repayments cannot be further reduced, you then need to see if there is any financial help you might be entitled to in making the payments if you can't manage them yourself. A good place to start is with the *social security system*. Although it sometimes seems dauntingly complicated, the social security system gives you a legal right to help when it is needed and you shouldn't hesitate to use it. Each year homeowners lose millions of pounds in potential benefits simply by overlooking their social security entitlements.

If you are in *full-time work* (normally treated as 24 hours a week or over) and have dependent children, you might qualify for the benefit *family credit.* This is available both to couples with children and single parents and it provides a regular weekly income top-up for periods of 6 months at a time. It doesn't have to be paid back and qualifying is fairly easy. To see whether you might be entitled, pick up the free leaflet FB4 *Cash Help While You're Working* from your local post office. The post office can also supply the family credit claim form FC1, a pre-paid envelope and an illustrative guide to what you might qualify for. Alternatively, you can phone free of charge to Freeline DSS on 0800 666 555 and they will send you the forms. Making a claim costs nothing and the benefit is not just for those on very low wages or with large families. Depending on your family size you could be earning as much as £10,000 a year and qualify. Although family credit will not provide any money specially geared to meeting your mortgage commitments, most people on the benefit are awarded more than £20 per week, which certainly goes some way to helping with the household budget.

If you are *not* in full-time work – because you only work part time or do not do any paid work – you might qualify for *income support* which does provide special help with making mortgage repayments (see below). Your entitlement depends on what other money you have coming in every week and how much you have in the way of savings. It is worked out by allowing an amount for your needs, those of dependant family members and extra 'premiums' depending upon your personal circumstances. If you want to discuss in confidence whether you might qualify you could telephone free of charge to Freeline DSS on 0800 666 555 or you could call in at an advice centre such as a Citizens' Advice Bureau (see page 130 for addresses or look in your phone book under C).

Alternatively, you could just make a claim and see what happens. It costs nothing to claim and you can either get a claim form B1 from the local Unemployment Benefit Office (if you are unemployed and signing-on) or claim form A1 from your local Social Security Office (in all other cases).

There is a whole host of other social security benefits which you may be entitled to and which could boost your weekly income. I cannot set them all out here but a simple general guide is given in free leaflet FB2 *Which Benefit?* available from your local main post office. Two good general guides are the *National Welfare Benefits Handbook* and the *Rights Guide to Non-Means-Tested Benefits* both published by Child Poverty Action Group. Your local library should have copies.

What help does income support provide towards mortgage repayments?

The claim form for income support asks you to give details of your housing costs including your mortgage repayments. This is because, in working out if you are entitled, an amount will be included to meet housing costs as well as amounts for your other personal needs.

Not surprisingly, the benefit system does not provide you with money to pay off the capital element of your mortgage. Nor will it pay the premiums associated with endowment mortgage policies. What it will cover in whole or in part is the regular interest on your home loan including any interest on a remortgage (see page 22) or a second mortgage (see page 22) taken out to buy your home or repair or improve it. In most cases the award of income support will include the whole of the interest you have to pay but there are five situations in which you may get less than the full amount:

(a) Unless you or your partner are over 60, you will only get help with *half* of the interest payable in the first

30

four months of your claim. If you are still receiving income support after four months you will get any subsequent interest met in full, plus an amount towards any extra interest you have to pay on arrears accrued during the first four months. (This rule will not be applied if you are making a repeat claim within 8 weeks of an earlier award of income support or your partner or former partner has received income support within the last 8 weeks.) If as a result of this rule you fail to qualify for income support at all, make sure you claim again after four months and you will then have your full mortgage interest included in your assessment.

(b) If you have a *non-dependent* person living in your home, an amount may be deducted from your mortgage interest to represent the contribution that the non-dependant should be making towards your housing costs. No deduction should be made if you or your partner are blind or receiving attendance allowance.

(c) You may receive less than the full mortgage interest if your repayments are considered *excessive*. Your payments will be treated as excessive if your home is unnecessarily large or unreasonably expensive. You can avoid the reduction if you can show that it is not reasonable to expect you to move. If you were able to afford the mortgage when you took out the loan, benefit cannot be reduced in this way for at least 6 months. You may be allowed a further 6 months without reductions if you are actively looking for cheaper accommodation.

(d) If you were receiving income support as a *sitting tenant* and have bought and now own that home, your interest payments will be limited to the equivalent of the rent previously used to work out your earlier housing benefit payments. This restriction will last until your housing costs increase again or until your family circumstances change.

(e) If you use your home partly for *business* purposes,

you are only entitled to interest payments in the proportion that your personal use of the property as a home relates to the property as a whole. For example, if 80% of your home is used for business purposes you only qualify for help with 20% of the interest repayments.

You can normally only get help with mortgage repayments on one property at a time but there are exceptions to that rule, for example where you are moving between properties and are liable to make payments on both.

If you disagree with any decision made about your income support entitlement you have the right of appeal free of charge to an independent tribunal. The organizations mentioned on page 131 could help you with an appeal.

I am already in arrears with my mortgage payments, what should I do?

This depends on what stage your lender has reached in taking action against you to enforce the loan. (If you have already received a letter from the lender's solicitors or notice of court proceedings, go straight to the next question.)

You will either have received, or will soon be receiving, letters from your lender notifying you that arrears have accrued and asking you to correct the position. Do not ignore these letters. Make an appointment to see someone in the lending organization. Explain the difficulties you are having and invite them to consider one of the ways of reducing your mortgage as explained on page 25. Put your request in writing or confirm your meeting by letter so that you have a record of the fact that you tried to co-operate at the earliest stage. Even if they agree to reduce your future mortgage repayments in one of those ways, you will still need to clear the arrears. There are several ways you might set about doing that:

(a) If you can afford it, offer to make regular monthly

payments to clear off the arrears over and above your future mortgage repayments. Most responsible lenders will allow you to do this over a period of months or years if you approach them while arrears are still at a fairly low level and you can show that you will keep to the arrangement.

(b) If you can't afford to clear the arrears in the near future, ask that they be added to the mortgage itself. This is technically called 'capitalizing the arrears'. What it means is that your regular payments will be higher or your mortgage period longer because the arrears have been added-in to the debt you already owe. You then have a fresh start and no arrears. You will need to persuade your lender that your house is worth enough to cover the increased amount of your debt and that you will be able to afford the new repayments.

(c) If your circumstances are definitely going to change for the better in the near future, ask your lender if repayments or collection of the arrears can be deferred for a short time. A lender will usually agree to do this if you will soon be able to clear the arrears in a lump sum (such as when you receive a redundancy payment) or by regular payments (such as where you start a new job).

(d) See whether you can claim any backdated social security benefits or more money from your present benefit. The main benefits which can boost your income are described on page 28. If you realize that you could have been entitled for some past period put in a claim now and ask for it to be backdated. If you are successful you can get up to a year's worth of back payments and this will help to clear the arrears. If you are already on benefit get your benefit checked by a specialist adviser, for example at a Citizens' Advice Bureau (for the address, look in your phone book under C), to see whether you are entitled to more.

(e) If you are already receiving income support, tell your lender that you agree to the DSS making the mortgage interest payments direct to the lender rather than to you. This will guarantee a regular payment. If you feel you can manage, you could also agree to the DSS paying a small part of your regular personal income support direct to the lender towards the arrears. Because this will mean your living on a very low income for some time it is worth taking advice before putting forward this option either to your lender or the DSS.

(f) If you bought your home from a local authority or housing association and you have little prospect of clearing the arrears or managing future payments, ask if the council or association would be prepared to buy your home back from you and grant you a fresh tenancy.

If none of these options work or apply to your circumstances and your lender is not willing to come to an arrangement that you can afford, DON'T STOP PAYMENTS. Work out how much you can definitely pay on a regular basis towards your current payments and/or your arrears and carry on paying that regularly. It will stand you in good stead if the lender presses on with enforcing the loan and in the meantime the lender is very unlikely to refuse your payments, however small.

What if I have received a solicitor's letter or court proceedings have already been started?
Don't panic. You are still a long way from losing your home. Whatever you do, DON'T BORROW MORE MONEY to pay off the debt you owe. You might be tempted to do this by the sort of newspaper advertising headed 'All your debts cleared'. This usually means you end up owing more than you ever owed before and have to repay it at exorbitant rates of interest. And DON'T ABANDON YOUR HOME – this will probably prevent your being rehoused by a local authority and will do nothing to help you clear the debt.

The best thing to DO at this stage is to get professional advice – and that may be available free or at a reduced charge. An organization called *Housing Debtline* specializes in giving free advice and assistance to homeowners in financial difficulty. Their address is, 318 Summer Lane, Birmingham B19 3ERL. If you ring them on 021 359 8501 they will send you a free fact sheet on how to deal with mortgage arrears and court proceedings. They answer the telephone on certain evenings each week so that you can make a cheaper call after 6 p.m. You could also get free advice and help from a local consumer advice centre on Citizen's Advice Bureau (page 130 has more details).

If your lender is likely to press ahead with court action, you could get cheap but good advice from a local solicitor. Some participate in a 'fixed fee interview scheme' under which you pay a small amount for up to 30 minutes' advice. Also, you can get free or reduced rate legal help under the 'green form scheme' which is part of legal aid (see page 132). Finally, if you are on a low or modest income you might qualify for legal aid to pay for a solicitor to represent you if your case has to come to court. Telephone or visit your local Citizens' Advice Bureau and ask them for the telephone numbers of local solicitors who take on this sort of work.

While you are seeking out advice and considering your position, you will need to negotiate for more time. Write to your lender's solicitors and say that you want to negotiate arrangements to clear the arrears and meet your current payments. They will agree to postpone any further proceedings if you make realistic proposals or are able to make regular payments towards the loan during any further delay. If the solicitors won't allow more time, approach the lender direct and explain that you are taking advice about your position and will be able to work out a reasonable settlement, given a little more time. They can instruct their solicitors to postpone further action.

With your adviser you should then have time to work out an arrangement with the lender which can resolve the dispute.

What happens if the case for repossession comes to court?

There will be a hearing, usually in private, at the local county court. It is absolutely essential that you attend because your home is at stake. If possible get a representative to help you at the hearing (see above for how to go about this). The case will usually be heard by a registrar. The lender will be asking for an order for possession of your home. There are several alternative things you could ask the registrar to do which would prevent your losing your home, even if it is agreed that you are in arrears:

(a) Ask for a *postponement* of the hearing. You should do this if you have not previously discussed your position with your lender or entered into negotiations or taken proper advice. The registrar is more likely to agree if you just ask for a short period (say 21 days) and you promise to pay something towards your loan during the postponement.

(b) Ask for *Time to Pay*. The court has power to suspend your lender's right to take possession of your home if you can show that there is a prospect of your clearing the arrears over a reasonable period as well as keeping up future repayments. The court decides what would be a reasonable period over which you should clear the arrears. It could be as long as the original mortgage agreement itself but most courts look at a one or two-year period. The court then works out, having regard to your income and prospects, whether you will be able to clear the arrears over that time by regular monthly instalments. If it is satisfied that you can clear the arrears, the court will suspend any possession order for as long as you keep up the arrears repayments and your current payments. The court might even be prepared to accept an offer of repayments over a fixed period, even one which your lender has already rejected.

(c) Ask for *Time to Sell.* If you are satisfied (after taking advice) that there is no way you can clear the arrears or keep up future payments, ask the court to defer the possession order to give you time to sell the house yourself. You will probably be able to get a better price for your home than the lender will if they sell it (usually at auction).

If an order for possession is made against you and not suspended, the registrar will tell you the date on which you have to leave. If you have not left by then the lender will arrange for a court bailiff to evict you at a later date. Once your home is vacant the lender will sell it, recoup money for the amount outstanding on the mortgage and for their costs and expenses, and pay you the balance.

If you lose your home in this way see chapter 8 (Finding a New Home).

I realize I will no longer be able to meet my mortgage repayments, what should I do?

Make sure that you have considered the possibilities for reducing your payments and increasing your income as described on pages 25–32. If possible get some advice about your situation from an organization like Housing Debtline (see page 35). Then, if you are still sure that you can no longer manage, you should consider selling your home yourself rather than wait for the lender to take action against you for arrears. If you bought your home from a council or housing association, write to ask them if they would buy the property back from you and grant you a tenancy instead.

If you are unable to sell or cannot afford to buy

another home, turn to the section on homelessness (pages 123–4).

Can I get any help with mortgage arrears by approaching my local council?

Even if your mortgage is not with the council, they may be willing to offer you some help if you face the prospect of loss of your home because of mortgage arrears. This is because, ultimately, they may have to deal with you if you are made homeless and, therefore, helping to prevent your homelessness may be an attractive option. Indeed, if you are within 28 days of losing your home and you are in a priority group (for example you have dependent children) the council must help you to try to prevent the homelessness arising.

One of the ways the council could help is by giving your lender a guarantee that they will meet any new mortgage or remortgage (see page 22) if you default. This might well attract a lender into agreeing arrangements to clear your debts, because they have nothing to lose – if you don't pay, the council will.

If your mortgage is with the local council, approach them at an early stage when you get into difficulties and follow the steps outlined at pages 25–6. They might even agree to buy back your property or enter into a shared ownership arrangement with you (see page 13).

Can I get help with payments under a rental purchase agreement?

If you have a genuine rental purchase agreement (see page 17) you can apply for housing benefit to help you meet the payments. Whether you qualify depends primarily on your income and savings. Most people on low or modest incomes are eligible. Your local Borough or District Council administers the benefit so ask at the town hall for a Housing Benefit Claim Form (for Private Tenants).

You might also be entitled to claim tax relief on your payments (although not through the MIRAS scheme described on page 24). Ask at your local PAYE tax office for more details. Their address and telephone number can be found in the phone book under Inland Revenue.

If you miss your payments, what happens next depends on the terms of the agreement itself. Ultimately, the owner can apply for a court order for possession. The court has power to postpone any possession case (or suspend an eviction order). The court will probably exercise this power if you can show that you will be able to resume regular payment and can clear the arrears over a reasonable period. If you face possession proceedings take legal advice immediately (see page 131).

What sort of regular insurance payments should I be making?

There are basically three types of insurance you are likely to have if you are a homeowner. They are: *buildings* insurance which covers the actual structure or fabric of your home; *contents* insurance which covers your personal possessions in your home; and a *life policy* which will meet any outstanding payments on a home loan if you die before the loan is cleared. This third type of insurance is described in more detail on page 23.

You probably first took out a *buildings insurance* policy when you bought your present home. Your mortgage lender may well have suggested the particular insurance company you took out a policy with. In order to ensure that you keep up the regular premium payments your lender probably collects them from you once a year (or in monthly instalments with your mortgage payments) and forwards them to the insurer.

If you are a *freehold* owner, buildings insurance is crucially important to you. If your home is damaged or destroyed it will provide you with the money to repair or rebuild your home. But an insurance company will only pay the full amount of any claim if you had your home insured for an amount which represented the full cost of rebuilding. This is not the same as the amount for which your home could be sold or for which you could buy an equivalent home. It is a figure representing what it would cost to clear away the remains of your old home if it were destroyed, re-lay the site and reconstruct a new property in the same proportions as the old.

This has two important implications for you. First you must make sure the you really are insured for an amount that represents the full rebuilding costs. If you expect (probably rightly) that this sort of cost goes up year by year then you need to make sure your cover also goes up year by year. To save you the trouble of making your own adjustment each year some policies are 'index-linked' and are increased automatically in line with the House Rebuilding Cost Index prepared by the Royal Institution of Chartered Surveyors. Check whether your policy has this facility.

Second, if you add a garage, build an extension or make other improvements to your home, that will obviously increase the rebuilding cost figure. So make sure you tell the insurance company so that they can increase your cover accordingly.

If you are not sure what the rebuilding costs for your type of home would be, write to the Consumer Information Department of The Association of British Insurers, Aldermary House, Queen Street, London EC4N 1TT for their free leaflet *Buildings Insurance for Home Owners*, which contains a cost guide.

If you are a *leaseholder*, your lease might well require you to reimburse the whole or part of the annual premium which the lessor of your home pays to maintain insurance on your building. If you are one of several lease-holders in a block of flats this is obviously a sensible arrangement as it enables the lessor to insure the whole block and apportion the costs of doing so among the residents. Because some freeholders in the past have not acted responsibly over buildings insurance (for example by not insuring for the full amount or simply not paying over the premiums collected) an Act of Parliament passed in 1987 gives you the right to check that the lessor of your leasehold house or flat has, in fact, taken out and paid for proper insurance. You just write to the lessor (or managing agent) asking for a written summary of the current insurance of the building. Within the month you should receive in reply: the name of the insurance company; the amount insured and the risks insured against. The lessor could send you a copy of the policy instead of this information. Failing to respond to your request is a criminal offence. Once you have these basic details you have a right at any time within the following 6 months to ask to see the full insurance policy for the current and past year and the receipts which show that the premiums have been paid. Again, a lessor refusing to provide this information is guilty of another criminal offence. For help in enforcing these rights see pages 131–3.

Sometimes your lease might require you to take out an insurance policy yourself with a named insurance company or one nominated by the lessor. If you don't like the insurance company chosen by the lessor you can apply to the local County court for the judge to appoint a different company. You could do this, for example, if the insurer chosen required excessive premiums or was in some other way an unsatisfactory or unreasonable choice. For help in enforcing this right see pages 131–3.

Once you are satisfied that the structure of your home is adequately insured you need to check that the *contents* are properly protected by insurance. It is worth checking the terms of your policy from time to time to be sure that all your valuables are adequately insured and that you have the right sort of cover. Some policies meet the full cost of replacing stolen or destroyed items, but others take into account wear and tear and therefore pay out lower amounts. You can get some useful tips on insurance from the free leaflet, *It Might Never Happen But* . . . at the Office of Fair Trading at Fields House, Bream Buildings, London EC4 01 242 2858) or from your local consumer advice centre or Citizens' Advice Bureau. Other useful free leaflets include *A Guide to Home Contents Insurance* and *Claiming on Your Home Insurance Policy* from the Association of British Insurers (for address, see above).

If you have a dispute about your insurance policies, whether for buildings or contents, take the matter up in the first place with the insurance company. If their local office is unwilling or unable to help, write to the senior manager at Head Office. If you still get no satisfaction, contact the Insurance Ombudsman Bureau at 31 Southampton Row, London WC1B 5HJ, or take advice from one of the places mentioned on page 130.

Do I have to pay general rates on my home?

General domestic rates were abolished in Scotland in April 1989 and will be collected for the last time in England and Wales for the financial year 1989/90. After April 1990 the community charge (or 'poll tax') will have replaced general rates everywhere and will be payable by, and collected from, individuals irrespective of property ownership (for that reason Community Charges are not dealt with hereafter in this book).

Do I have to pay 'ground rent'?

Ground rent is an annual charge you may have to pay if your home is owned on a lease. Your lease tells you what amount you have to pay and when you have to pay it. Payment is made to the person or company from whom you lease your property (your lessor) or their agents.

Ground rents are usually quite low, perhaps £50 or £100 per year, but it is important they are paid. The lease will usually say that if the ground rent is not paid on time the lessor can go to court for an order to bring the lease to an end.

If the lessor writes to you for the ground rent rather than expecting it to be paid automatically, the notice or demand must show the lessor's name and address. This is so that you will always know how to get in touch with them if there are any difficulties.

If you fail to pay the ground rent your lessor might start court action against you. If this happens you could take advice from one of the places mentioned on pages 130–1 but if your home is at risk it may be best just to pay the ground rent and the court costs so as to avoid losing your lease.

You may qualify for financial help with meeting the ground rent if you are on a low or modest income. If your lease is for more than 21 years, the social security office will give you money towards your ground rent if you receive income support (see page 30). If your lease is for less than 21 years, you can get help through the housing benefit system administered by your local council. Ask at the local town hall for a Housing Benefit Claim Form for Rent.

Do I have to pay 'service charges'?

If your home is owned on a lease you might have to pay regular service charges to the person or company from whom you lease your property (the 'lessor'). The lease itself describes the items the lessor can charge for. These will vary, depending on whether your home is a leasehold house or leasehold flat. The lease will also show what proportion of the lessor's total costs you have to pay and when payments are due. Service charges are rarely mentioned in leases as fixed amounts. More usually the lease provides a formula (perhaps in a schedule) from which the lessor can work out how much of the costs can be passed on to you in the form of service charges.

It is quite possible that the lease requires you to pay the service charge in advance of the provision of the services themselves. If so, it probably also says what will happen if the eventual cost of the services turns out to be more or less than you have paid.

When you receive a written notice or demand for service charges, check it carefully. First, make sure the person or company demanding the money is in fact the current lessor. Second, if the demand contains a break-down of what the service charge is for, check your lease to see that only those things mentioned in your lease are being claimed. Third, check that the demand is asking you for the right proportion of the total cost. Fourth, check the arithmetic – everyone makes mistakes. Fifth, see if the demand is for charges incurred recently or long ago – the lessor can only claim for charges incurred in the past 18 months unless you have had written warning that a late bill would be coming.

If you feel the charges claimed are unreasonable you might be able to challenge them (see page 46). If you find that the cost of major works is being claimed for, the lessor may not be entitled to recoup those costs (see page 47). If there is any reason why you are not happy with the service charges, it may well be worth mentioning the matter to the residents' association to see if others share your concern. Because there have been lots of problems about service charges in the past few years, the legal rights of leaseholders have been considerably streng-thened. I give some of the details in the following pages but there are very useful free booklets for leasehold flat and house owners called respectively, *Service Charges in Flats* (Housing Booklet No.10) and *The Rights & Duties of*

Landlords and Tenants of Houses (Housing Booklet No.26), which you can pick up from a local Citizens' Advice Bureau or other advice centre.

Can I get more information about my service charges?

Yes. In the past, some demands for service charges have been very vague. You may have found it very difficult to understand what the lessor was claiming for. As a result of recent changes in the law, you now have the legal right to full details about your service charges. You are entitled to a written summary of the costs incurred in the year up to the presentation of the claim for service charges or the last complete service charge year. You get the information by writing to the lessor either direct or through his or her managing agents. Failing to supply you with the summary without a reasonable excuse is a criminal offence.

If there are more than four leaseholders contributing to the service charges, the summary the lessor sends you must be certified as a fair and accurate summary by a qualified accountant.

Of course, the summary will be based on the actual bills and invoices that your lessor has incurred in providing the relevant services. If you suspect that some figures in the summary are over-inflated or otherwise unreasonable you could take advantage of a new legal right to see the actual documentation on which the summary is based. All you have to do is write to the lessor (or managing agent) within 6 months of getting the summary. The lessor must then make arrangements so that you can inspect all the paperwork and (at a reasonable charge) take photocopies. Again, if the lessor fails to provide these facilities he commits a criminal offence. If you need help in enforcing these rights take advice from one of the places mentioned on pages 130–1.

What should I do if I feel that my service charges are unreasonably high?

First, check the accuracy of the demand in the way described on page 44. Second, get a copy of the free leaflet *Service Charges in Flats* (Housing Booklet No.10) or *The Rights & Duties of Landlords and Tenants of Houses* (Housing Booklet No.26) from your local Citizens' Advice Bureau or other advice centre. It explains exactly what to do if you think the charges are unreasonable. Third, raise your concerns with any residents' association – you may find that other leaseholders have a similar response to their demands and you will find it easier to challenge the charges if you act as a group. Fourth, exercise your rights to more information described above so that you have got chapter and verse about how the charge was worked out. Then consider whether you want to challenge the service charges as being *unreasonable*. Under recent Landlord & Tenant Acts, you are only liable to pay for expenses 'reasonably incurred' and for services or works of a 'reasonable standard'. If you feel you are being charged excessively or for slipshod work or poor services, write to the landlord enclosing your payment of that part of the service charges you consider reasonable and explaining why you are not paying the rest (keeping a copy of your letter). If your case rests on the failure to provide a proper service (for example if the lessor is charging for lift maintenance and repair but the lift is constantly out of action), make sure you have good records to support your case (for example a note of when the lift was out of service, when you reported it and how long it took before it was repaired).

Your letter will probably produce a reply from the lessor asserting that the charges are reasonable. From then on, in what will probably be a series of letters or telephone calls (of which you should keep copies or notes), you can try to reach a compromise with the lessor on what you both agree would be a reasonable settlement. You might find it helpful to involve the residents' association in the negotiations – indeed it may be willing to negotiate on your behalf.

If the dispute cannot be resolved by negotiation it will have to go to court. At this stage you will definitely want to take legal advice (which might be arranged for you through the residents' association). See page 131 for how to go about getting legal advice.

Can the lessor get me to pay for major building work as part of my service charges?

Sometimes the repair or maintenance needed on a property will involve extensive, major and therefore expensive work and your lessor may seek to recover the cost from you as service charges. Your first reaction must be to check your lease to see whether this sort of charge is permitted. Until recently, if the lease said you had to pay – then that was it, even if you had not been consulted about or approved of the major work.

Recent laws now regulate claims by lessors for the cost of major works. These are currently defined as works costing more than £1000 as a whole or £50 per dwelling (but the Government can raise these thresholds from time to time). Unless the lessor follows the legal procedure, he or she cannot recoup the cost of the works above those amounts by way of service charges. The procedure involves the lessor notifying you (or a recognized residents' association for your property) what works are proposed in advance of them starting. The notice must have attached two estimates for the cost of the works and must either be copied to you or be displayed prominently in the building. The notice must invite you to submit comments on the proposed works to the lessors and allow you a month to do so. Unless the works are very urgent, they cannot be started until the consultation period has closed and the lessor has considered any comments you have made. Obviously, the purpose of this procedure is to give you some 'say' in the conduct of major works for which you have to ultimately pay by way of service charges. If it is not followed the building costs incurred by the lessor cannot be recovered from you.

What happens to the money I pay in service charges?

Hopefully, it is properly used to meet the reasonable costs of the services provided under the lease and any surplus is refunded to you or any shortfall requested by a supplementary demand.

Regrettably, in the past there have been instances where work paid for in advance is not carried out and lessors just retain the service charges. To remedy this the law now provides that if two or more leaseholders are paying service charges for the same costs or services, the lessor must put the monies in a separate trust account until they are paid out to meet the actual costs and expenses. This trust money has to be invested and the interest it makes is added to the trust fund. Any surplus after the expenses have been paid out is redistributed to the leaseholders in proportion to what they paid in. The great advantage of the new system is that whatever happens to the lessor, the trust fund will be there to ensure that the necessary services, etc. can be provided.

Can I get any financial help with my service charges?

If you are in financial difficulties you may find a demand for service charges an extra worry – particularly if the demand is for a large amount or a substantial increase on previous years. Check that the demand is in order in the way described on page 44. Remember that your obligation to pay is one between you and your lessor. If you have a responsible lessor, write to him explaining that you are in temporary difficulties and offer to pay in instalments.

If your lease is for a period of less than 21 years and you are on a low or modest income, you could get help towards some or all of the charges by claiming housing benefit from your local council. Ask at the town hall for a Housing Benefit Claim Form for Private Tenants.

If your lease is for more than 21 years the housing benefit scheme cannot help but the social security system might be able to. You should make a claim for the benefit income support (see page 28 for how to do this). In working out how much you are entitled to each week the social security office takes into account the amount of any service charges you have to pay. There is no maximum amount of help you can get in this way. One homeowner recently got a £17,000 service charge bill covered by income support!

3: Your Home and Your Family

What rights have members of my family got to live in my home?

If you are the sole owner of your home, it is largely your decision who lives there with you. Because you are the sole legal owner, everyone else's rights to be in the home depend on you. If you are married, your spouse has legal rights to be there too (see page 55) even if she or he is not the joint owner. Sometimes, but very exceptionally (see page 54), other members of your household have the legal right to live in your home.

If you jointly own your home (for example with your partner) then all the joint owners have the right to live in the home and to decide together who else should live there. If you and the other joint owner(s) cannot agree which of you should live in the home, see below.

In this chapter, I consider what rights other people have to live in your home and how they can enforce those rights. The chapter also covers other aspects of using your home as a family home.

What if my home is jointly owned and I and the other joint owners cannot agree which of us should live in it?

Hopefully, you and the other joint owners will be able to resolve the difficulty by discussion and negotiation. Perhaps you can occupy part of the home and they the other part or you have it some parts of the year and they others. If you cannot agree, then the legal position is described below if the joint owner is your spouse special rules apply and I describe these on page 51).

The basic rule is that joint owners all have the legal

right to occupy the property. No one joint owner can sell the property without the permission of the other(s). If one is shut out by the others he or she could get a court order to get back in.

Therefore, if you are unable to reach agreement with the other joint owner(s) there are only two ways forward: either one of you buys the other out or you have the home sold and the proceeds divided up between you. If neither of these options is agreed by all the owners then any one of the joint owners can apply to a court for an order that the house be sold and the proceeds be divided up.

This type of difficulty most commonly arises when a family relationship between two joint owners breaks down or where one of the joint owners becomes bankrupt (and the official referee or trustee in bankruptcy wants the property sold in order to realize money to pay the creditors) – see page 56.

If you can afford it, you might want to buy out the other joint owner(s) and keep the home for yourself. There is plenty of information about how to raise the money on pages 19–21. If you cannot afford to buy out the other(s) or they will not sell to you, the problems may result in your losing your home, so it is well worth getting legal advice (see page 131). If you are on a low or modest income you may qualify for legal aid to help you meet any legal fees (see page 132).

What if the other joint owner is my spouse?

The first thing to consider is whether you want to carry on living in the same home by perhaps arranging your affairs so that you live separately and independently. This basically involves maintaining two separate households under the same roof. An arrangement like this will **not** prejudice your chances of later getting a divorce on the grounds of 'separation'.

If this possibility doesn't appeal, you should see if you

can reach agreement about which of you will carry on living in the home and what the financial arrangements will be.

Another alternative to consider would be that you could 'buy out' your spouse's part of the home. Your spouse is likely to agree to that only if he or she is content to leave the home and the money you offer will be enough to finance alternative accommodation.

If you cannot agree, then either of you could apply for a court order that the house be sold and the proceeds divided up.

If you or your partner is going to apply for a divorce or judicial separation, the court will have power to rule on which of you should live in the home and whether it should be sold. This is described in more detail on pages 55–6. The judge could also order the transfer of your property out of your joint names into one name only.

Obviously, at or before this stage you should take legal advice (see page 131). If you are on a low or modest income you could qualify for Legal Aid (see page 132) to help you meet the legal fees.

If you are not legally married to your partner (i.e. you are just living together) your position is as described in the answer relating to any joint owners.

Whether you and the joint owner are actually married or live together as husband and wife, either of you could apply to the court for a temporary order excluding the other or simply to get back in. See page 53 for the details of these 'domestic violence' orders.

If I am the sole legal owner, does that mean I can tell other members of my family to leave my home?

With the exception of the position of your spouse (explained on page 55) the general rule is that you have the absolute right to ask any members of your family or household to leave your home. In law the other people who share your home as members of your household (cohabitees, children, other relatives, lodgers, etc.) do so with your permission. The law would describe them as licencees. Because your 'permission' for them to be there has never been formally written down, they would be described as your 'implied licencees'.

If you want them to leave it would only be fair to warn them and give some advance notice. Technically the law would require you to give 'reasonable notice' but there is no legal minimum time limit. If they refuse to go, you don't need a court order to evict them – you can just wait for them to go out and then not let them back in. However, it is probably not a good idea to resort to physically ejecting them yourself. It might be better, if they refused to leave, to call the police or get a court order.

Of course, it would only be very rarely that you would ask a member of your own family to leave your home or think about involving the law or legal proceedings. But it is possible that your lodger or another member of your household is causing difficulties or has perhaps turned violent and refuses to go even after you have asked them to leave. In these circumstances you should be able very easily to get a court order at the local county court to have that person evicted from your home. You probably won't even need a lawyer, although you should take some advice from one of the places mentioned on pages 130–1.

If the person you ask to leave has been living with you as husband or wife (although you are not legally married) he or she has the right to apply to the local county court for an order enabling him or her to stay on or, indeed, to exclude you. Because you are the sole legal owner, such an order would only be short term. These sorts of orders are most commonly made where there has been domestic violence. A similar order could be made in a magistrates' court. If there is a child of the relationship, your partner could apply to the county court for an order transferring your home to the child or to your partner to provide a home for the child. If you receive notice of these sorts of applications to courts, take legal advice urgently (see page 131).

Very exceptionally, even though you are the sole legal owner, other people in your family might have acquired the legal right to live in your home irrespective of your wishes. Such a person is said to have an 'equitable right' to live in your property. Because these equitable rights are rarely written down, they are quite hard to identify. You can get some idea of the type of thing which counts as an equitable right from the following examples:

(a) A man bought a house from his elderly mother in his sole name. This was at a reduced price and the agreement between them was that she would carry on living in the property as her home with him until she died. A few years later her son tried to evict her. Although the agreement between them was never written down, the courts decided it gave her an equitable right to live in the house for the rest of her life which the courts would enforce.

(b) A man bought a house in his sole name to provide a family home for his new partner and her children from a previous relationship. He told her it was to be the family home and that she could live in the house for as long as she wanted. Relying on these promises the woman moved in and gave up her own previous home. Later the man tried to have her evicted. She was said to have an equitable right to stay in the home.

As you can see, the courts tend to identify these equitable rights where the fair thing to do seems to be to allow the family member the permanent right to stay on in the home.

What rights does my spouse have to live in my home?

If the two of you have lived together in the property as your matrimonial home, your spouse has very considerable rights to carry on living here, even if you are the sole legal owner.

Under the Matrimonial Homes Act your spouse has the legal right to occupy your home. If you try to take that right away by eviction or locking him or her out, your spouse can get a court order forcing you to let him or her in again. Indeed the Act even gives your spouse power to apply for an order evicting *you* (but that would only be granted in very exceptional circumstances).

If you try and defeat your spouse's rights to occupy your home by putting it up for sale, your spouse could prevent your completing the sale by registering his or her legal right of occupation against the official records held for the property (see page 14).

Obviously if you want properly to overcome your spouse's right to live in your home you will want to take legal advice and seek a court order ending his or her rights of occupation, probably in the context of ending your marriage.

What happens to my home if I am married and my marriage breaks down?

Your home becomes treated as one of the 'assets' of your marriage just like all your other possessions and property. Hopefully, if your friendship is going to continue, you and your spouse will be able to agree what should happen to your home.

If you cannot agree or you are going to go for a divorce or judicial separation, then the courts will decide the future of your home. If there are children involved a very typical court order would be: that the home should be occupied by the children and the parent with care and control of the children until the youngest child reaches 18 or finishes school, with the house then being sold and the proceeds divided between the former spouses.

If you or your spouse are considering a divorce, the position about what happens to your home and other property is well explained in the *Divorce Handbook* published in this series and available from libraries and bookshops.

Does a 'cohabitee' have the same rights as a spouse?

If you have been living with someone as husband or wife (your 'partner') he or she may have some legal rights to stay in your home (or exclude you) but these rights are not usually as strong as they would be if you were legally married. If your partner owns the home jointly with you, then the position is as described on page 50.

If you are the sole owner, your partner can apply to a court for an order excluding you and/or reinstating them in the home. Magistrates' courts and county courts can grant such orders if there has been violence between you, but the county court can make such orders in any circumstances. Because you are the sole legal owner, your partner will only get an order lasting a short while to give them time to make other accommodation arrangements. If there is a child of the relationship, your partner could apply to the county court for an order transferring your home to the child or to your partner (to provide a home for the child). If you receive notice of these sorts of applications to courts, take legal advice urgently (see page 131).

What happens to my family's rights to be in my home if I become bankrupt?

If you are declared bankrupt, your home, or your part of your home, will be taken over by the official referee or trustee in bankruptcy who will want to sell it to raise money and pay off your creditors (see page 106). If you have a family at home this may mean that your family risks losing their home.

If you were only part owner of your home with another member of your family, then the trustee in bankruptcy becomes a co-owner in just the same way you were. The position about disputes between co-owners is described on page 50. Ultimately, if your co-owner cannot afford to buy out the trustee in bankruptcy, the trustee can apply to the court for an order that the property be sold and the proceeds of the sale be divided up.

If you were the sole owner of your home when you became bankrupt, then the members of your family face a very real risk of losing their home and both you and they urgently need to seek legal advice (see page 131).

What happens to my family's rights to be in my home if I die?

That largely depends on you. If you have decided that a particular member or members of your family should have the home after your death, you should reflect that decision by making a will. This can be done simply and cheaply (some stationery shops sell blank will forms), but if you see your home as a valuable asset and you want to make sure your intentions are achieved you could employ a solicitor to draft a will for you. In your will you appoint an executor who becomes responsible after your death for ensuring that your wishes are carried out and that the ownership of your property is passed to the person you have specified.

In most cases, the decision which you reflect in your will cannot be disturbed after your death, even if it might upset some members of your family. There is, though, one exception: if you had people dependent upon you at the time of your death and you were maintaining them, they could apply to a court to overturn your will if you had made insufficient provision for them. For example, a dependent spouse or children could challenge your will if you left them nothing and gave your home to a charity.

If you don't leave a will, when you die the ownership of your property will pass under what are called 'laws of intestacy'. These provide a ranking-order of your next of kin and specify how much of your estate (including your home) each of them receives. Usually the operation of these rules means that any surviving spouse (or, in the absence of a spouse, children) takes over the whole or part of your home.

4: Repairs and Improvements to your Home

What repairs or improvements can I carry out to my home?

As the owner you will usually bear the responsibility of maintaining your home in good condition and seeing to the need for repairs. It will be up to you what improvements, if any, you make and when you do them (but see below). If you own your home on a lease, that will usually set out exactly which matters you are responsible for and which are the responsibility of the person or company your lease is with (the 'lessor'). The lease might even require you to pay service charges (see page 43) which contribute towards the cost of any work the lessor does. If the lessor is not honouring his repair obligations you could force him to do so (see page 71).

Obviously it is in your own best interests to carry out maintenance and minor repairs around your property in order to keep it in good condition and therefore comfortable to live in.

However, you may have bought a home in poor condition or, for some other reason, need to do expensive repair work. Or you might want to make some improvements or adaptions to your home. This chapter looks at the restrictions (if any) imposed on the type of works you can do and the sources of finance available that might help you meet the costs. If you want more general information about home improvements write to the Office of Fair Trading, Field House, 15–25 Breams Buildings, London EC4 1PR (01 242 2858) for their free 12 page booklet, *Home Improvements*.

Can I be forced into carrying out repair work against my wishes?

If you own your home under a *lease* you will be bound to carry out any repairs which are said to be the lease-holder's responsibility under the terms of the lease. Check through your lease to see what sort of repairs you will be obliged to do. If your lease was granted originally for a period of less than 7 years, there is a law which overrides the lease and means that the lessor has to do most of the repairs – if this applies to you, see the section on repairs in the *Private Tenants Handbook* in this series and ask your local Citizens' Advice Bureau or advice centre for a copy of the free leaflet *Repairs* (Housing Booklet No.20). In all other cases you must do the repairs required by the lease. If you fail to do them, the lessor could take action against you and ultimately ask a court to take away or 'forfeit' your lease. It would mean you losing your home. If you need financial help with meeting the costs of the repairs your lease requires you to do, see pages 63–7.

If you own your home *freehold* rather than under a lease, it is largely up to you whether you carry out repairs, although in the following situations action can be taken against you if you don't repair your home:

(a) *Buying on a mortgage* – mortgage lenders sometimes make it a condition of the loan that, within a certain period of moving in, you carry out repairs. These will usually be the most serious items identified in the valuers report which the lender commissioned before advancing you the money. It would be unwise simply to ignore these repairs even though some lenders are quite lax about following up loan conditions. If you need more time to do the work, write to your lender and ask for an extension of the time. If you need financial help see pages 63–7.

(b) *Compulsory repairs notice* – if the local authority for your area (usually the District Council) becomes concerned over the condition of your property, it will ask you to take remedial action. This might be because your home is in very serious disrepair and as a result it is unfit or in unsatisfactory condition. Your contact will usually first come in the form of a visit or letter from an Environmental Health Officer. It is worth responding positively to such an approach as the EHO can offer helpful advice about financial assistance with the cost of repairs and if you take no action in response to a visit or letter the local authority could serve legal notices on you forcing you to do repair work. Although you have rights of appeal, any failure to do the work might lead to a penalty and the council could do the work themselves and charge you their full costs. If you need financial help with the cost of the necessary works see pages 63–7.

(c) *Listed building* – if your home is of particular historic or architectural interest it may be 'listed' by the Secretary of State for the Environment. This will mean you have a duty to keep the property in good repair and condition. You could be forced to do any necessary repairs but there is usually entitlement to grants and other financial help. See pages 63–7 for more details.

(d) *Dangerous buildings* – if your home falls into such a condition that it becomes a hazard to passersby or neighbours, the District Surveyor could serve notice on you requiring sufficient repairs to make the building safe. If you fail to do the work you may be penalized and the work will be done and the full costs recovered from you.

(e) *Homes which are a nuisance* – even if your home is not a hazard, it could be in sufficiently poor condition to amount to a nuisance to your neighbours – for example, if your gutters leak into their garden or your roofslates slip into their yard. Although they could take this up with you themselves, the Environmental Health Officers from the local council (see above) have powers to serve legal notices under the Public Health Acts forcing you to stop the nuisance by doing any necessary repairs to your home.

Could the condition of my property mean that I lose my home altogether?

Yes. If your home has fallen into such poor condition that it is unfit to be lived in, the local council through its Environmental Health Officers could take action against you. If they think the cost of putting the property right would be unreasonable they can serve on you a 'time and place' notice requiring you to attend a meeting to discuss what will happen to your home. They will have in mind that you should be ordered to demolish the property or at least stop using it as a place to live in. You should definitely go to the meeting if you get such a notice. If possible, get advice before doing so. You could get a builder or surveyor to estimate the cost of the works to be done and persuade the council that you will in fact carry out the work. If the council do not accept what you propose, they could make a Demolition Order (or if your home is needed to support others – because it is a flat or in a terrace – a Closing Order). You have a right of appeal and if you have not already done so before that stage you should certainly take legal advice if you receive one of these notices.

Another way the council can deal with your property if it is unfit is by forcing you to sell it to them under a compulsory purchase order (see page 101).

Other circumstances in which the condition of your property might cause you to lose your home is if it is structurally unsound, subsiding or has been damaged by an act of God. These matters are dealt with on pages 97–101 in chapter 7 (Losing Your Home).

If you own your home on a *lease* and you neglect your obligations to carry out necessary repairs you not only risk loss of your home through action taken in one of the ways described above but there is also the possibility of the lessor taking action against you for breach of your obligations under the lease.

How can I finance necessary repair and improvement work?

There is a great deal of repair and improvement work which qualifies for help in the form of grants from the local council. There is more information about these grants on page 65 and you should certainly consider applying for any that appear appropriate because in most cases they do not have to be repaid. However, none of the grants will cover the whole cost of the work you want to carry out, so you will need to consider covering at least some of the cost yourself or from other sources.

If you have sufficient savings to pay for required work yourself, all well and good. See if you can save some of that by qualifying for a grant but remember that you must apply for the grant and have it approved before you start the work. Also see page 69 as to whether you need permission to do the proposed work.

If you don't have sufficient savings to finance the work, you need to raise the necessary money in other ways. One obvious source would be the lender who originally helped finance the purchase of your home. You may even still be paying off that homeloan. If you are happy with the services provided by that lender you could ask for a top-up of your original loan or a new additional loan (sometimes called a second mortgage – see page 22). Most banks, building societies and other responsible lenders are happy to lend further money for repair or improvement works which increase the value of the property on which their loan is secured – all the more so if the bulk of the work is being paid for by a local authority grant. If your original homeloan is in the MIRAS scheme (see page 24) it is worth asking for the new loan to be separate rather than a top-up of your original loan. This is because loans for repair and improvement work no longer qualify for tax relief. If such a loan were a top-up of your original loan, it would take it out of MIRAS and you would have to make your whole mortgage and loan repayments gross and later reclaim tax relief from the Inland Revenue. If you are refused a loan by your present lender or you would prefer to try elsewhere, you could try a different lender or lending institution for the new loan. Do approach this with care. Loans made for short periods (such as ordinary bank loans) can be at very high rates of interest. To keep repayments down to a reasonable level, you could ask for the loan to be spread out over a longer time. You will need to give details of not only the work you propose to do but the value of the property against which the loan will be secured and the income from which you will be making repayments.

Obviously, you will want to check that you can manage the repayments before you accept the new or increased loan. If you are on a low or modest income (or your income falls after you have taken out the loan) you can get help with the loan if you qualify for the benefit income support (described on page 30). If you receive this benefit you could apply for a community care grant or budgeting loan (see below) to meet any surveyor's or other professional costs you have incurred in arranging the loan for the repair or improvement work. The income support rules will also mean that you get help with the 'interest' part of the repayments on your loan. This only applies to certain types of repair and improvement work and is available whether you took on the loan before or after you claimed income support. Check with the local social security office that your type of loan is, or will be, covered by the rules.

If you are claiming the benefit income support when the need for repair or improvement work arises, consider two possible options before taking out a commercial loan – these are the community care grant and the budgeting loan. They are both administered by the Social Fund Officers based at your local social security office. The application form is the same for both (Form SF300) but the best one to go for is a community care grant because that does not have to be repaid. There are few legal rules about the circumstances you have to fulfil in order to qualify for a grant – the Social Fund Officer looking at your application has considerable discretion and is helped by guidance issued by the Department of Social Security. You are most likely to qualify if you can show that if the work was done on your home it would reduce the risk of your having to leave your home and move to a care home, hospital or some other institution. You could also get the grant if the work is necessary to improve the safety of your home, especially if you have young children or disabled people living with you. If you are refused a grant it is worth applying for a review of that decision. One of the agencies mentioned on pages 130–1 could help you with this. The alternative help available from the Social Fund Officer is a budgeting loan. You must be getting income support and have been receiving it for six months before you apply. If you are granted the loan it will be interest free (which makes it more attractive than a commercial loan) and it will be repaid by making deductions from your weekly benefit.

What grants can I get towards the cost of repair or improvement work?

The local authority for your area (normally the District Council) has wide powers and, in some cases, duties to make grants available to homeowners to meet the costs of repairs and improvements. The grants are usually administered by the Housing or Environmental Health Department of the Council. You can get the address and telephone number from the local town hall. They will send you the application forms on request and will probably visit your property before making a decision on the application. At present it costs nothing to apply so in most cases it is well worth making an application. The one slight snag is that the council might require you to do additional or different work to that which you had in mind. In certain circumstances (see page 60) they might actually have power to compel you to do the work.

The council might also ask you to have plans drawn up before they consider your application. If you have to pay additional costs (for example surveyor's or architect's fees) you can add those costs to the amount you are seeking a grant for.

Whatever you do you must not actually start any of the work before a decision is made on your grant application otherwise you may well lose a grant to which you would otherwise have been entitled.

At the time this chapter was written the legal rules about grants were under review by Parliament. This was because the grants scheme had become too complicated (with at least six different types of grants) and the rules were confusing. For a good summary of the up to date position pick up the free leaflet *Home Improvement Grants* (Housing Booklet No.14) from your local Citizens' Advice Bureau or other advice centre. It will set out all the new rules about grants.

If your home has a major structural defect and you bought it from a public authority you might be entitled to a grant under a different system which I explain on page 100.

Is there any special help for the elderly or disabled homeowner?

Yes. Local Social Service Departments have a duty to help with essential repairs and improvements for elderly or disabled homeowners (or for homeowners who have elderly or disabled persons living with them). That help might take the form of arranging the work for you, helping you to pay for it or arranging a grant from the local

District Council. You can get in touch with the Social Services Department at the offices of your County or Regional Council.

They will initially send a social worker to visit you at home and perhaps later an 'occupational therapist' specially qualified to advise and assist on the sorts of adaptions or improvements available. You will then get a decision about the type of help the Social Services Department are prepared to give. If you are not happy that this fully meets your needs, write to the Director of Social Services and ask for your circumstances to be reconsidered. If you still don't get all the help you think you should receive contact your local county councillor and ask him or her to take up your case.

Another organization committed to assisting the older or disabled homeowner is Care & Repair Ltd. They can provide help and advice about paying for improvement work and in some cases give direct assistance in making applications for grants, arranging loans and organizing repair work. Their address is 175 Gray's Inn Rd, London WC1H 8UK (01 278 6571). The older homeowner will also find much of assistance in *Owning Your Home in Retirement* and other publications from Age Concern, 60 Pitcairn Road, Mitcham, Surrey CR4 3LL (01 640 5431).

What is the best way to choose a good builder or contractor?

There is no guaranteed way of finding a good builder or contractor. If you decide to employ someone to do the work for you, then there is always a certain amount of risk, but there are some tips which can help you reduce that risk.

First, take advantage of the free advice and inform-ation available about choosing a reliable contractor. The Office of Fair Trading (address on page 59) have a useful free leaflet called 'Home Improvements'. If your area has a Consumer Advice Centre, call in there to see if they have local information about reputable contractors. The section of your local authority which administers home improvement grants (see page 65) probably has a list of local contractors (especially builders) both recommended and not recommended.

Second, shop around. Approach the relevant federation of contractors or craftsmen of the type you need (for example the Federation of Master Builders, see page 129) and ask for a list of local members. Then from the list pick two or three and ask them to visit in order to give you estimates for the work.

Third, supplement the information you already have by considering whether any particular contractor has a reputation for good work in that area. Ask the contractors you might consider employing to give you names and addresses of two or three other customers they have worked for in the area so that you can go and see their workmanship for yourself. Perhaps your neighbours, friends or relatives have used a particularly good contractor.

Fourth, be precise about exactly what work you want done and the time within which you want it done. Make a list of what needs doing in advance and copy it so that each of the possible contractors can have a copy when they visit to assess the job. If you are going to have a lot of work done it is worth thinking about employing an architect, draughtsman or surveyor to draw up a specification of works for you.

Fifth, consider carefully the estimates you receive. Make sure they cover all the works you have asked for. Beware if the response you receive is headed 'Estimate'. That means exactly what it says – the builder estimates the work might cost that much, but if it turns out to cost more then you might have to pay more. What you want is a fixed price or 'quotation' so that you can know exactly what you are going to pay. This should clearly indicate the VAT element in the total cost.

Finally, settle your agreement with the contractor in writing. A responsible contractor will probably have a set of standard terms and conditions attached to a full schedule of the works agreed. If your contractor doesn't have that, make sure you have something in writing before the work starts, showing what work will be done, what materials will be used, how long it will take, when payment is to be made and what reductions in payment you will be entitled to make if the job runs over the agreed time.

Do I have to get anyone's permission before starting work?

If you own your home on a *lease*, the lease itself will probably place restrictions on the work you can do to your home so you need to check its terms carefully before starting work. Often it will have clauses preventing you doing certain work without the lessors consent, in which case you should write to the lessor or managing agent for his agreement before you go ahead. If the lessor refuses to agree to the sort of work you want to do and you want to go ahead, take legal advice before doing so (see page 131).

If you are the *freehold* owner it may be worth your checking the deeds of your property before you go ahead with any work. This is because the deeds often contain promises ('covenants') made to adjoining landowners about how your land will be used or built on. The work you propose (particularly if it is some additional building such as an extra garage or extension) might contravene one of these covenants which could ultimately mean your being forced to pull it down at your own expense.

If your home is a *Listed Building* (see page 61) you must obtain special Listed Building Consent from the local planning authority before you can start any work on the building itself.

Aside from these rather special situations, the only general restrictions on what you can do to your own home are those contained in the Planning and Building Laws which apply to all properties. You can quite easily check whether the work you have in mind needs planning permission (or approval under building regulations or by-laws) by reading the free leaflet *Planning Permission: A Guide for Householders* available from your local Citizens' Advice Bureau or other advice centre. If you are still in any doubt, contact the Planning Department of your local council for advice. It is well worth checking and double checking whether the work you are proposing requires permission because, if it later appears that you do need permission and it is refused, you may be forced to reinstate your home as it was before, at your own expense.

What does it mean if a Renewal Area is declared for a district which includes my home?

A local authority can declare a Renewal Area for a particular district in order to make improvements to the land, buildings and environment in that area. Such action used to be undertaken by declaring Housing Action or General Improvement Areas but the Renewal Area has taken the place of these. If your home is in a Renewal Area this may have important implications for you. On the one hand, it could mean more grants are available to help you improve your property and carry out necessary repairs and it could lead to a general improvement in the environment of the district in which your home is situated. On the other hand, the declaration of a Renewal Area gives the local authority important powers (including the power of compulsory purchase) over land and buildings within the Area. For more information about the ways in which you might be affected by the declaration of a Renewal Area ask at the Environmental Health Department of your local District or Borough Council.

What can I do if my lessor refuses to repair my home?

First check that your lease actually makes your lessor responsible for the type of repair work that needs to be done. Some repairs could be your responsibility under the lease and other repairs might not be mentioned at all (in which case you will have to agree who is going to do, and pay for, the work).

Next, make sure your lessor knows of the need for repairs. Write to him or his managing agents with details of the disrepair (keeping a dated copy of your letter). If this produces no response contact your local District Council and ask for an Environmental Health Officer (EHO) to visit your home. These officers have power to serve legal notices on lessors requiring them to carry out works which are their responsibility. There is no charge for the services of an EHO.

If these steps produce no result or the lessor takes an unreasonably long time before starting work, you will become entitled to compensation. You can claim this compensation (and an order that the landlord must do the works) by starting a legal claim in your local county court. You will want to take advice about this type of claim and you may qualify for legal aid (see page 132) to help you pay any lawyer's fees.

If you live in a flat or in one of a group of houses, and you find that your lessor is taking no proper interest in the property and is not carrying out necessary repairs, it is worth raising your concerns with any residents' association for your estate or district (the address of the Federation of Residents' Associations is on page 9). Through the Association, or even on your own, you could apply to the local county court to have a 'manager and receiver' appointed to take proper care of your home. The court-appointed manager will collect the ground rent and service charge instead of the lessor and see that the lessor's responsibilities are properly carried out. Usually the manager would be a responsible person you have suggested to the court (such as a qualified surveyor). Again, you will want to take advice from one of the places mentioned in chapter 9, before applying to the court.

The ultimate sanction available to leaseholders of flats with neglectful lessors is the compulsory transfer of the lessor's title to the property to the leaseholders themselves. If a majority of leaseholders are agreed, a local county court can make an order forcing the lessor to sell out to the leaseholders or to someone nominated by them. Effectively the homeowners then manage their own homes. The conditions for the court making such an order are that either a 'manager and receiver' (see above) has been in post for three years or it is not practicable to have a 'manager and receiver' (e.g. because insufficient monies are collected by ground rents and service charges to finance the repairs needed). If you think this might be an option in your case, canvas the opinions of your neighbouring leaseholders and take advice from one of the places mentioned in chapter 9.

5: Letting Your Home or Parts of Your Home

What are the various ways that I might let other people live in my home?

If you decide to let someone else take over the whole of your home while you move out and you charge them money, then you are normally granting a *tenancy* of your home. In this chapter I call this *letting out your home*. You might want to do this because you are going to work overseas or you will for some other reason be away from home for some time. The person will be your *tenant* because you will be granting them the sole use or possession of your home for a fixed period (or perhaps a recurring period such as from month-to-month or week-to-week) and be charging them rent. The law recognizes these factors as creating a tenancy. If you make this arrangement with several people at the same time they become *joint tenants*. If you make separate arrangements with different people at different times (for example one uses the upstairs part of your home and the other the downstairs part) then you are creating several different tenancies.

Alternatively, you might decide to let someone move into occupation of part of your home (such as a bedroom, flatlet or converted bed-sit) while you carry on living in the rest of the house or flat. If they have their own use of that part of your home and pay you money for it they are your *tenants* of that part. In this chapter I call this situation *taking in a tenant*. The law recognizes this arrangement as one of tenancy because the new person will have exclusive use of some part of your home and will be paying you rent either over a fixed period or on a recurring basis. You will not be free to come and go in the room or rooms you have let out to them.

A third possibility is that you bring someone into your home to live as part of your household. This could be a friend or relative or complete stranger. You probably give such a person the use of a bedroom in your home, they share the use of the rest of your home with you and they contribute to the cost of their keep. In this chapter I call this situation *taking in a lodger*. The law recognizes this sort of an arrangement as a *licence* because the person has your permission to be in your home but they are not tenants because you are free to come and go in and out of 'their' rooms and they live as part of your household. You are likely to enter into this sort of arrangement if you supplement your income by taking in lodgers or students or because you need a live-in carer or home-helper.

For more detail on the distinction between a tenancy and a licence see the *Private Tenants Handbook* published in this series.

What steps do I need to take before letting out my home or taking in a tenant or lodger?

The most important thing to bear in mind is that someone else will be making their home in your home. The law will probably confer on them some rights and protections arising from that. You may, therefore, find that when you want them to leave they have temporary or permanent rights to stay. This will not only affect your own use of the property but also its value if you try to sell.

It is therefore in your own best interests to get advice about letting out your home or taking in a tenant or lodger before you let anyone move in. Even what seems to be a sensible informal arrangement with a friend, relative or someone recommended to you can turn sour and leave you with very serious legal problems.

In the rest of this chapter I outline some of the rights and responsibilities which arise in situations like these. You can get an idea of all the relevant issues from the free booklet *Letting Rooms in Your Home* (Housing Booklet No.22) available from local advice centres such as the Citizens' Advice Bureaux.

If I let out my home, how can I be sure of getting it back when I need it?

In order to encourage you to keep your home in use rather than empty when you have to be away from it, the laws about protection for tenants are relaxed so that if you let out your home you can be sure of getting it back when you need it.

To take advantage of these special provisions as an owner-occupier you have to give a written notice to your tenant before you grant the tenancy. This tells the tenant that the property you are letting can be repossessed under 'Ground 1' of the grounds for repossession because you are an owner-occupier. Although the courts have power to waive a failure to issue the necessary notice, it would be more sensible to get the notice right (see below) rather than rely on the discretion of the court. If the tenant leaves and you decide to take on a new tenant, the same rules apply about giving notice before the start of the fresh tenancy.

You and the tenant should then agree the terms of the tenancy itself covering such matters as the length of the letting, rent, how it can be increased or decreased, repairs, etc. If you are letting the property furnished you will need to agree an inventory of the items in the home and their condition.

Many homeowners considering this type of letting get help with drafting the notices, agreement and inventory from professional advisers such as lawyers or property managing agents (at least the first time round). Or you could do it yourself by buying a 'kit' of documents from law stationers such as Oyez, 49 Bedford Row, London WC1.

The type of tenancy you have granted will be a variety of the assured tenancy. This type of tenancy is intended to give some rights to the tenant while protecting your rights to your home. You can get more details from the free leaflet *Assured Tenancies* (Housing Booklet No.19) available from Citizens' Advice Bureaux and other advice centres. The leaflet also describes an arrangement called the assured shorthold tenancy which you may prefer to use, depending on your individual circumstances.

When you decide you want to bring the tenancy to an end, you may want to give the tenant as much notice as possible. Perhaps you have decided to return home or the tenant has proved unsatisfactory. Whatever informal notice you give, you must also send the tenant a formal notice to start the process of bringing the tenancy to an end. There are technical requirements about these notices and the types of notices which must be served are prescribed in regulations for most assured and assured shorthold tenancies. You should therefore get advice from your solicitors or managing agents about what the notice should contain. Alternatively, the details are outlined in the free leaflet *Notice That You Must Leave* (Housing Booklet No.24), available from your local Citizens' Advice Bureau or other advice centre.

If the tenant does not leave when the notice expires you will have to go to the local county court for a possession order. If you have served all the necessary notices and can produce copies to the court you should have no problem in getting a possession order reasonably quickly. The tenant could be ordered to pay your legal costs as well as some element of compensation for not having moved out when he or she should have done. You don't have to give the court any special reason for wanting your home back – indeed you might just want possession so that you can sell it for a better price.

(The rules I have just described are slightly different if

you let out your home before 15 January 1989.)

If I take in a tenant, can I be sure my tenant will leave when I ask him or her to go?

Usually the answer is yes. In order to encourage home-owners to make use of spare rooms in their homes the laws which protect tenants are relaxed if the landlord is a 'resident landlord'. This makes it easier to get possession of the rented room or rooms. This is also because, although there are always problems if the relationship between landlord and tenant are not good, those problems can be much worse if both are living in the same property whether it be a large house converted into flats or a small apartment.

The general rule is that if you ask a tenant in your home to leave and he or she does not do so you will be guaranteed the granting of a possession order by the local county court. The only requirement is that you give your tenant a notice to quit in the proper legal form. You can get details about this from the free leaflet *Notice That You Must Leave* (Housing Booklet No.24) available at a Citizens' Advice Bureau or other advice centre, or ask your solicitor or managing agent.

Obviously, in order to claim the benefit of these relaxed rules you may be asked to prove to the court that you have in fact been occupying the same building as the tenant and have had your home there throughout the tenancy.

It is even easier to get repossession if you and your tenant have shared use of some 'accommodation' in the property which is your home. For example, where you and the tenant share the use of a living room, kitchen, bathroom or WC. In order to get possession against this sort of tenant you only need to bring his agreement to an end (by whatever notice the agreement stipulates) and he must then leave at the end of the notice period. There are no other legal formalities about what needs to be contained in the notice. If he refuses to move out, you could just take back the rooms which are the subject of his tenancy. In practical terms it might not be sensible just to change the locks or to try and exclude him in some other way as this may lead to confrontation and possibly violence. If you go to the county court for a possession order you may find this sort of unpleasantness avoided.

(The rules I have just described are slightly different if you had taken in a tenant before 15 January 1989.)

When can I ask a lodger to leave?

Your lodger is entitled to receive reasonable notice if you want him or her to leave. There is no legal definition of what is 'reasonable notice' but most licencees (which is what lodgers are – see page 74) now have the legal right to a minimum of four weeks' notice and a proper legal notice to quit containing specific information (the details are contained in the free Government leaflet – *Notice That You Must Leave* – Housing Booklet No.24). If your lodger does not leave at the end of the notice period you will need to apply at the local County court for a repossession order.

Again, there is an exception to this general rule if you and your lodger have had the shared use of some part of your home such as a bathroom, WC, kitchen or lounge. In these circumstances your lodger does not need to be given a formal notice to quit, just reasonable verbal notice to leave. If he has not left by the end of the time allowed, you can simply take back the room he has occupied. You could do this by just changing the locks or forcibly evicting him but this tends to lead to situations of unpleasantness or violence which can best be avoided simply by applying to the County court for a repossession order which will be automatically granted.

(The rules I have just described are slightly different if you took in a lodger before 15 January 1989.)

How much can I charge?

Laws about how much tenants can be charged have been very much relaxed in the last few years. In any of the situations I have described above, you are free to agree whatever initial charge you think is right. Obviously, if you pitch your price too high you may find it difficult to attract anyone and you also need to bear in mind the financial implications of the income you will receive (see pages 81–2).

In most cases it is sensible to write in to the initial agreement you draw up with your tenant or lodger some provisions about the payments going up or down during the period that he or she will be living in your home. This will avoid unnecessary disputes and renegotiations every year. You could say, for example, that the rent will increase every year by the rate of inflation as at a given date.

If you don't have anything in the agreement about rent increases it will be up to you to raise the matter with your tenant when you think a rise would be appropriate. If the tenant agrees with you or you come to a compromise then the new agreed rent will become the rent payable. If you cannot agree, you serve a formal notice on your tenant (you can get details from a solicitor or property agent) increasing the rent. If the tenant doesn't like the increase and cannot persuade you to agree to a smaller increase, the dispute can be referred to an independent Rent Assessment Committee. That committee can set a maximum rent at what it feels would be the reasonable market rent for the property. You will be bound by this figure for a year unless you can persuade your tenant to pay more. The rules are slightly different if you have granted the type of tenancy called an assured shorthold tenancy (see pages 75–6). Under that sort of arrangement the tenant can apply to the Rent Assessment Committee to reduce the rent to market levels if it is unnecessarily high.

Obviously if there are continuing difficulties or disputes over rent you could ask your tenant to leave and you may be able to repossess his or her part of your home in the ways described on pages 75–9.

Who is responsible for things like repairs and insurance?

As it is your home that you are letting the whole or part of, you remain responsible for major repairs and the insurance of the property. If you have let out your home and are living elsewhere this may mean you have two lots of buildings and contents insurance at each address (see pages 39–42). Your tenant will expect you to see to necessary repairs and has the legal right to require you to correct any problems with the structure or exterior of the home or any of the installations in it (such as the baths, washbasins, etc.). Obviously, you are not responsible for repairing any damage done deliberately by the tenant, but you must see to any items that are damaged accidentally or by wear and tear.

Do I need anyone's permission before I let out my home or take in tenants or lodgers?

Most homeowners are free to make their own decisions about letting all or part of their homes. This is because they have the legal right to control who uses the land and buildings. There are two main exceptions to this general rule.

First, if you are buying your home on a mortgage you should check the terms of the mortgage to see if there are any restrictions on you taking in tenants or letting out your home. You may find that the mortgage requires you to get your lender's permission before letting. This works as a safeguard for the lender who might otherwise find the value of the property on which the loan is secured very dramatically reduced by the presence of a sitting tenant. Many homeowners ignore or overlook their obligations to inform mortgage lenders and very few lenders regularly check up on whether their properties have been let.

Second, if you own your home on a lease you should check what the lease says about letting all or part of your home. Look for phrases like 'sublet', 'part with possession' and so on. The lease might say that you have to get the lessor's permission for subletting. If you take in tenants or let out your home without getting that permission you will be in breach of your lease.

More details about these and the other implications of letting are given in the *Private Tenants Handbook* available in this series.

What are the financial implications of taking in tenants or letting out a home?

The money you receive from tenants or lodgers will be income. Obviously, therefore, you will have to declare it on your tax return each year and pay income tax on it. You will not have to pay tax on the full amount as deductions are allowed for the necessary costs you have associated with renting, such as small repairs, cleaning, etc. You can get a good idea of the deductions allowed from the booklet *Notes on the Taxation of Income from Real Property* (IR 27), available from your local inland revenue PAYE office (address in the phone book under Inland Revenue).

If you are in receipt of income-related social security benefits such as income support, family credit or housing benefit, the income you receive from tenants or lodgers will obviously affect your benefit but the rules are quite generous to stop you losing one pound of benefit for every pound you receive from tenants or lodgers. Allowances are made for the costs you have associated with letting. However, you should always make sure you inform the benefit paying authorities as soon as you take in a tenant or lodger or let out your home. Not only will this mean your benefit is correctly calculated but also that you avoid any unnecessary personal questions which might arise if the authorities find out from someone else that there is a person living with you in your home. If you want to check what effect renting all or part of your home would have on your benefits you can telephone a social security official for advice free of charge on 0800 666 555. Alternatively call in at a local advice centre or Citizens' Advice Bureau.

If I decide to employ a managing agent to take care of arrangements for me, how do I pick a good one?

There is no easy way to be sure you are selecting the best available managing agent but you might find it helpful to follow these tips. First, make sure you have a selection to choose from. Ask friends or neighbours for recommendations and get names and addresses from newspaper advertising or the telephone directories. Second, try to identify agents who have professional qualifications (in law or valuation) or who are members of some professional body (such as the Royal Institution of Chartered Surveyors or the Association of Residential Letting Agents) and who have experience. They ought to be able to mention other customers who would be prepared to recommend their services. Third, find out what you can about the agents by visiting their offices and have them call at your home to view the property and discuss their services. Fourth, invite three or four agents to give you full written details of the services they provide and the charges they make. Finally, when you have selected the one you prefer, make sure that the terms of your agree-

ment with them are written down – either in one document or in an exchange of letters between you.

Before you even start your search you should be clear
exactly what you want the managing agent to do. This
might range from simply finding possible tenants to actually collecting rent, serving notices and seeing to repairs.

What if there was already a tenant living in my home when I bought it?

If you thought you were buying the property with vacant
possession but you find a tenant in residence, you obviously need to take legal advice urgently. Start with the
solicitor who acted for you in the purchase but if it
becomes clear that it might be their fault that you have a
sitting tenant you may need to take other legal advice (see
page 131).

If you bought the property without satisfying yourself
that it was vacant or without legal advice, then obviously
you may be bound by the existing tenancy. You could
approach the vendor for an explanation, but probably the
best thing to do is take legal advice immediately.

Where you knew there was an existing tenancy all well
and good. You should contact the tenant as soon as the
purchase is completed and let them know that you are the
new landlord. You need to provide your name and
address and let the tenant know where to make future
rent payments. You will probably have got full details of
the tenancy itself from the person who sold you the
property.

Whether you can increase the rent or ask the tenant to
leave depends on the type of tenancy they have. This in
turn depends on when the tenancy was granted, the terms
of that tenancy and whether you and/or the person you
bought from have been living in the same building as the
tenant or shared accommodation with them. Because
tenancy laws have undergone so many changes in recent

years it really is essential to get advice about the exact position very soon after you complete the purchase of your home. Try one of the places mentioned on pages 130–1 or take legal advice. Under no circumstances should you try forcibly to evict the tenant or deliberately make life uncomfortable for them in your home. Such action can amount to a breach of both criminal and civil laws and lead to severe financial and other penalties.

What if I return home to find a complete stranger in occupation?

Unless you gave the person permission to be on your property, they are trespassers and must leave when you ask them to. Most genuine squatters (those living in other people's property because they have no home of their own) will peacefully move on if satisfied that you really are the resident homeowner. If any of your property has been damaged you could ask them to compensate you or call on the police for help (an offence of criminal damage will have been committed).

If the people in occupation refuse to leave, the quickest way to have them removed may be by calling the police. This is because if a person refuses to leave property after having been asked to do so by the resident homeowner they commit an offence of criminal trespass and can be arrested by the police. If the police are not prepared to get involved (perhaps because you can't immediately satisfy them that you are indeed the owner-occupier of the property) you have two remedies: one practical; one legal. You could wait until the trespassers leave the house (to go shopping, for example) and then let yourself back in, breaking in if necessary (after all it is your own property), and then secure the property by changing the locks, etc.

The remedy offered by the law is an immediate order for possession from the County court judge. You should go as soon as possible to the local County court and explain to the officials that you want to use the squatters' procedure (mention 'Order 24' and they will understand what you mean). They will explain what steps you need to take and give you a date when you can come back (only a few days later) for your application to be heard. If you follow the correct procedure you will almost certainly be granted an order for immediate repossession.

If these procedures mean that you temporarily have nowhere to live and you are unable to arrange your own accommodation you should apply to the local council. They must accept you as homeless if you cannot get into your own home and if you are in a priority group (for example if you have children or are vulnerable) they must arrange temporary housing for you. There is more advice about homelessness on page 123.

6: Your Home and Your Neighbours

Where is the boundary between my property and my neighbour's property?

This question is more frequently asked by the owners of houses than by those who have flats. But giving a clear answer is as difficult in both cases. It *should* be fairly easy to find out where the boundaries of your property lie by looking at the title deed or the lease on which your home is held. This will usually (but not always) have a map or diagram attached, indicating the boundaries of your property. The problem is that these maps or diagrams are very rarely carefully drawn and almost never to a detailed scale. As a result, a homeowner can often have difficulty accurately identifying where the boundaries of the property actually lie.

If your home is within an area of registered land (see page 14), the boundaries of the land will have been recorded by independent officials for the Land Registry when the title to your home was first registered. They will have noted the exact positions of walls and fences and there will be a Land Certificate showing your home, and the land surrounding it, drawn to scale. This should show where the boundaries are and, hopefully, corresponds to the map or diagram attached to the title deeds of the property. However, even this detailed diagram will not show the boundary to within a greater accuracy than a foot or so either way.

To save endless disputes over the boundaries between various plots of land the law adopts a rule that a boundary which has been present and unchallenged for 12 years is the correct legal boundary. This can have important implications if you find a neighbour moving a wall or fence over what you think is the boundary and into your land. If you ignore the matter the new practical boundary will become the new legal boundary after 12 years. Try to agree between yourself and your neighbour where exactly the boundary lies. If you are unable to agree take legal advice (see page 131).

Am I responsible for maintaining the walls and fences around my home?

It should be possible to answer this question by referring to the title deeds for your home or the lease on which your home is held. This will hopefully spell out precisely which, if any, of the walls and fences around your home are your responsibility. Of course, it is usually only the walls or fences around the boundary of your property that give rise to any doubt because clearly any you erect within the boundaries of your own property are your own responsibility.

If your home is a flat held on a lease, the walls and fences around the building containing your flat are unlikely to be your responsibility and more likely that of the freeholder of the property.

In the case of boundary walls and fences around a house, the normal rule is that the responsibility is with the person who erected them (and their successors). In modern times, land developers have imposed duties to build or maintain walls and fences on the purchasers of the property by including these requirements in the title deeds. The plan attached to the deeds should show the wall and fences on at least one side (and perhaps the back) of the property to be your responsibility.

Older housing, particularly of the terraced type, may have one or more 'party walls and fences'. This means that you share responsibility with your neighbour for the wall or fence itself but can do what you want to your own side, for instance, grow creepers on your side of a fence or erect shelving on your side of the wall. If the wall or fence needs repair or replacement, then when and how this is done is a matter for you and your neighbour to agree and you will share the expense.

If you are going to carry out works to a wall or fence for which you are solely or jointly responsible, don't overlook any restrictions which may apply. Your lease or title deeds might impose conditions (see page 69) about the type of materials used, the height of the wall, etc. You could also check with the Planning Department of the local council to ensure that there are no planning conditions which may limit your intentions – planning conditions are much more likely to restrict what is erected on or close to the boundary between your house and any highway. Don't forget also that you must avoid interfering with your neighbours rights to light (see pages 92–3). In almost all cases it makes sense to let your neighbour know what works you propose to undertake if the wall or fence also marks their boundary.

Can I force my neighbours to repair walls or fences for which they are responsible?

Ironically, you may be more likely to get a positive response from a neighbour that is a public corporation rather than from an individual. This is because some public bodies (in particular the Railway and Highways authorities) are under legal duties to repair their fences so as to prevent accidents occurring on their property.

If your neighbours are not willing or prepared to accept their responsiblity there may, in practice, be little you can do. If they are leaseholders, you might complain to their lessor or freeholder and ask for action to be taken. If they are tenants of the council, a housing association or are privately renting, you might try writing to the landlord or property owner. If they are a homeowner, there may be a provision in their title deeds requiring them to maintain a boundary fence or wall. This is very likely if there is such a provision in your deeds and the properties were built at the same time. It might be worth pointing this out to your neighbours who may be unaware of the requirement. If you are unable to make progress through persuasion and negotiation you will have to seek legal advice (see page 131).

Are there things my neighbours can force me to do or prevent me doing?

Quite possibly, yes. You should certainly not take any action which interferes with your neighbour's rights of way (page 91) or their rights to light (pages 92–3) and you should avoid causing any nuisance (page 94). Beyond that, the only obligations that your neighbour can insist that you observe are any binding promises which relate to your use of your own property or which allow your neighbour some use of your property.

The type of binding promises which you must observe in your own use of your home are called 'covenants'. You will find details of any covenants in the title deeds of your home (or in your lease if you own your home leasehold). The most common type of covenants relate to your use of your home. For example, you may find a covenant to use your property for private residential purposes only or one preventing you from putting up any permanent buildings in your garden. These are called restrictive covenants because they restrict your freedom to do what you want with your home. Sometimes there are positive covenants; that is they make you do something, such as a covenant to keep your home in repair or prevent it becoming unsightly. If you own your home on a lease then both positive and restrictive covenants can be enforced against you by your lessor. Your neighbours could therefore ask the freeholder or lessor of your home to take action. If you fail to observe the covenants you may be at risk of forfeiting your lease (see page 106).

If you own your home freehold then the positive covenants can only be enforced by the person who sold the property to you (which is very unlikely unless they are a building company still developing a housing estate). But *restrictive* covenants can be enforced by any neighbours who have the benefit of those promises – probably also written into their deeds. So if you breach a restrictive covenant (for example by building an extension contrary to a restrictive covenant not to do so) your neighbour can take steps to enforce it against you. Ultimately this could involve them being granted a court order preventing you from doing what you want to do or requiring you to remove something you have constructed or erected.

The other type of binding promise is the one which allows your neighbour to do something on or over your land. This type of obligation is called an *easement* and again you will find the details in your title deeds. The most common easements are those granting your neighbour a right of way (page 91) over your property, a right to run a telephone line over your garden to a telephone pole or a right to support of their building by yours (see page 93). These easements can be enforced by your neighbours in the same way as restrictive covenants.

Can I get rid of any of these obligations that benefit my neighbours?

You could ask your neighbours to release you from any restrictive covenants (see above) of which they hold the benefit. Obviously, because the original promise is set out in the title deeds, you will probably need to take legal advice (page 131) about how exactly to make binding the agreement which releases you from the obligation. You may find a difficulty in establishing exactly which of your neighbours have the benefit of the covenant – especially if the land neighbouring yours has been divided into many sub-plots. You could ask your neighbours about this.

An independent body called the Lands Tribunal has the power to delete obsolete or unreasonable covenants from the title of property if you apply to them. You might want to do this if, for example, your home has a restrictive covenant preventing you from building an extension while all your neighbours have extensions. You can get the details of the procedures involved by writing to the office of the Lands Tribunal at 48 Chancery Lane, London WC2.

An alternative way of defeating these old restrictions on freehold property is simply to act in breach of them. If no one takes any steps to stop you the covenant will lapse by passage of time.

Does my neighbour have a right to go across my property and vice versa?

If you give your neighbour personal permission to cross your property, then obviously they can exercise that right until you withdraw it. In some circumstances your neighbour may have the legal right to go across your land with or without your permission – this is called a *right of way*. The existence of such a right of way should be shown in the title deeds of your home and/or in your neighbour's title deeds.

If there is nothing in the title deeds, the law will still recognize your neighbour as having a right of way in either of two situations. The first is where the only access to his property is by crossing yours. In this situation (called a right of way by necessity) the law is that there always was a right of way intended even though not written into the title deeds. The second avenue to establishing a right of way is by prolonged use. The normal rule is that if the right of way has been used as such for twenty years without interruption by the owner and without the owner's permission then it becomes established whether it is referred to in the deeds or not.

If you have just bought a home and someone starts using a right of way across your land, ask them about it in a friendly way and see if you can find out on what basis it is being exercised. If you want to stop it, take legal advice (see page 131).

My neighbour and I share the use of a passage or drive; who is responsible for it?

If you and your neighbour both have rights of way (see above) over a piece of property (perhaps the passageway running behind your homes), the general rule is that you and all the other users of the right of way are jointly responsible for its upkeep and maintenance unless the deeds specify which of the users (or an original owner) is responsible for the upkeep. A person who fails to make his or her contribution to the costs of repair, etc. is treated as losing their right of way until payment is made.

If you and your neighbour share a common driveway, the legal boundary of your property might run along the middle of it. Strictly speaking you are travelling over your neighbour's land when you use it. Accordingly, your title deeds should show the existence of mutually enjoyed rights of way and hopefully also make provision for the shared cost of maintenance. Otherwise, you and your neighbour only have responsibility for your respective parts of the drive.

Do I or my neighbour have 'rights to light' for our homes?

Such a right (to have natural light enter the windows of your home) might be written into the title deeds of your home or be acquired by passage of time. Generally the rule is that if you can establish that you have had light through a particular window in your home for more than 20 years, you have the legal right to restrain any unreasonable interference with the access of that light to your home. Obviously, it is possible to abandon the right to light for a specific part of your home by bricking up a window and making a new opening elsewhere.

There are many ways in which your neighbour might interfere with your right to light – from the wholly innocent (as where a tree on their property grows to such a height as to block or obstruct light to your window) to the intentional (for example, your neighbour erects a tall fence, large hoarding or building which prevents light entering your rooms). Obviously the first step is to point out the difficulty to your neighbour. If they are uncooperative you will need to take legal advice (see page 131).

If you are proposing to develop or extend your home, do remember that your neighbour may have a right to light which you should not interfere with. It might be that you are contemplating some such work in the future and want to ensure that your neighbour will not have acquired a right to light by the time you propose to start the work. If there is nothing in their title deeds and they do not have an established right to light from 20 years use, you could apply to the independent Lands Tribunal (see page 91) for a light obstruction certificate to prevent your neighbours getting a right to light. If you obtain this before the 20 years are up, you will prevent your neighbour acquiring a right to light for a further 20 year period.

Do I have a 'right of support' for my home?

If your home is a leasehold flat you will have rights of support for your home as part of your lease with the lessor or freeholder. If your home is a freehold flat see page 11.

If your home is a house you have an unlimited right to prevent your neighbour taking steps to destabilize your property. For example, if your neighbour excavates a large trench on his land undermining the support for your home, you have the right to take preventative action. If your neighbour doesn't voluntarily take corrective measures, you could get a court order requiring him to restore support to your home.

If your neighbours have a building which adjoins your home, you will not necessarily have a right to support from that building. You need to check your title deeds. If there is no right, then there is nothing to prevent your neighbours taking away or destroying their building provided they do not do any damage to yours or to any party wall (see page 87), indeed they probably don't even need planning permission. If your home begins to sink or sag as a result of the removal of the other building take advice urgently (see page 99).

What can I do if my neighbours cause a lot of noise or other nuisance?

You have the protection of law against acts of *nuisance*, that is, things that your neighbours do on their property which cause annoyance or harm to you in your enjoyment of your home. But obviously the first thing to do is discuss the problem with your neighbour who might be unaware of the inconvenience being caused.

If the nuisance continues and is unacceptable, then there are a number of steps you could take.

First, if your homes are held on leases, write to the lessor or freeholder complaining about the nuisance and asking for action to be taken. If the neighbour is a tenant of a council, housing association or other landlord write to them and ask them to control the actions of their tenant.

If your neighbours own their home, you will have to consider taking some action yourself. There are several useful free leaflets which explain the steps involved and these can be supplied by your local Citizens' Advice Bureau or other advice centre. The Camden Law Centre in London have a very straightforward one called *Stop*

That Noise (send an s.a.e. to 2 Prince of Wales Road, London NW5 3LG). Alternatively, ask for the free Government leaflet *Bothered by Noise? What you can do about it.* If the nuisance is one of noise or smoke, etc., contact the Environmental Health Officer employed by your local council (ask at the town hall). He or she will visit your home and will have the necessary equipment to measure noise. The EHO has powers to serve notices requiring your neighbours to stop the nuisance. If that proves ineffective you or the council can make a complaint to the local magistrates' court. As an alternative you could apply for an injunction in the local County court. The procedures are not complicated but because they involve using courts it is always wise to take advice first (see chapter 9).

The key to taking effective action to stop your neighbours' nuisance is to keep good records – both of the occurrence of the nuisances themselves and of the complaints you make to your neighbours. Make this as specific as possible by compiling a diary of events detailing not only the times and dates of the nuisance but also the extent (for example 'So loud we could not speak to one another without shouting').

Can my neighbours control how I use or maintain my home?

Beyond the various rights described earlier in this chapter, your neighbours are entitled to restrain you from using your property in such a way as to cause a nuisance to them. If you unreasonably cause noise or smoke or some other nuisance to interfere with your neighbours' enjoyment of their property they could take action against you in court both for compensation and for an order preventing any further nuisances. (In just the same way you can proceed against them – see the last question).

Public health laws also restrain you from using your property in an unneighbourly way. If you allow your home or premises to become dirty or dilapidated to such an extent that it might represent a health risk or a nuisance to your neighbours or the public, you are probably causing a 'statutory nuisance'. This might happen, for example, if your pipes or gutters overflow into the neighbouring property because they are blocked or broken. It is the job of local Environmental Health Officers (EHOs) to take action against homeowners who allow their premises to become a 'statutory nuisance'. If you are visited by an EHO it is a good idea to co-operate with suggestions made because, if an EHO is satisfied that your home amounts to a statutory nuisance, orders can be served which would lead to court proceedings if not observed.

7: Losing Your Home

Under what circumstances might I lose my home?
Like most people, you probably feel that owning your
own home is the best way of keeping it in your possession
in the long term. You may even be planning to pass it on
to the next generation of your family (see page 57). It can
come as a surprise then to consider just how many
circumstances might arise in which even a homeowner
can lose their property. In this chapter I cover the following ways in which a home might be lost:
(a) flood, fire or other disaster,
(b) subsidence,
(c) major structural problems,
(d) compulsory purchase,
(e) bankruptcy,
(f) family break up,
(g) repossession.
Unless your home has been destroyed in some disaster,
the key to keeping it is to get advice as soon as possible
when the prospect of losing your home arises. Many
homeowners lose their property every year simply
because they sit back and do nothing until it's too late.

There will be many other, perhaps more remote, examples of ways in which your home might be lost than those
I cover in this book. If you face the loss of your home for
whatever reason, follow the golden rule and take prompt
advice – either from your lender (if you are buying your
home with a mortgage or a loan) or from one of the
advice agencies mentioned in chapter 9.

What should I do if my home has been lost in a fire, flood or some other disaster?

The most immediate priority will be to get some alternative accommodation while you consider your options. Unless you prefer to make your own arrangements, you can approach the local housing authority for your area (usually the Borough or District Council). They have general powers to provide emergency accommodation and will use these if a large number of households have been displaced by the disaster – for example where a whole street of houses is destroyed or flooded. The authority will also be obliged to offer you personal help in getting accommodation under the laws which govern their duty towards homeless people. These are more fully described in the *Homeless Persons Handbook* available in this series. Unless you in some way caused the destruction of your own home, the council's duty will be to arrange that you are accommodated indefinitely in suitable housing. This might be permanently in council or housing association property or just temporarily until your own home is reconstructed, if you are going to be able to move back in.

Having arranged accommodation and placed such personal possessions as you have been able to recover into storage, you will next need to claim on your insurance. Two types of insurance are relevant. First, you will want to claim on your buildings insurance (see pages 39–40) for the cost of repairing or rebuilding your home. If you are not sure which insurer your buildings insurance is with, ask your mortgage lender or (if you are in a flat) the lessor. This claim will be for the cost of reconstructing your home or repairing the damage done to the structure.

Second, you will want to claim on your contents insurance (see pages 39–42) for the loss of your personal possessions and other items of property. This insurance might be with the same or a different insurer as the buildings insurance. If someone else was to blame for the destruction of your home the insurance company rather than you yourself will claim against them for compensation.

What should I do if my home is subsiding?

You might detect subsidence from cracks appearing in the walls of your home or tears in wallpaper. Perhaps even from cracking or creaking noises. The first thing to do is to get specialist advice. You should call in a qualified surveyor to establish whether subsidence is the problem, and if it is to suggest both a cause and a remedy. (See page 115 for how to find a good surveyor.)

If subsidence is confirmed, your next step will depend upon your personal circumstances. If you are buying your home on a mortgage, inform the mortgage lender and seek their advice. If you have very recently bought your home, you will want to know why your surveyor didn't spot the problem and will probably want to take legal advice (see page 131) about claiming compensation from the surveyor (see page 116).

If subsidence is related to the *foundations* or preparation of the ground before construction, you might have a claim for compensation against the original builder or developer who undertook the construction work. If the building was put up after 1st January 1974, those responsible for erecting it were under a duty imposed by the Defective Premises Act to ensure it was properly built. You can get legal advice (see page 131) about claiming compensation for the cost of putting the problem right.

If your home was built or converted within the last 10 years, a National House Building Certificate should still be in force for the property. You could contact the National House Building Council for help and advice. Their address is on page 128.

You should also consider whether the local authority for your area is in some way responsible. They will have approved the original plans and should have checked that the building was being properly constructed while the work was in progress. So a claim against the council might provide another way of getting the funds you need to put the problem right. Here again you will need to get advice (see pages 129–30).

If your surveyor advises that the subsidence may be related to current or past mineworking in the area you might be able to claim compensation from the National Coal Board. You can get more details from the leaflet *Coal-Mining Subsidence: How to make Claims* from your local NCB office or Coal Board showroom.

You should also check your Buildings Insurance policy to see whether it extends to damage caused by subsidence and if it does, put in a claim.

What if my home has a major structural fault?

Most houses and flats are built with a finite life-span, usually tens or (rarely) hundreds of years. It must be anticipated therefore that the 'life' of a property will eventually run out. That day can be long delayed by careful maintenance and repair work of the type described in chapter 4 (Repairs & Improvements to Your Home). However, some properties have developed or will develop structural faults which are so serious as to mean that they require very extensive reconstruction or can no longer be occupied. A qualified surveyor should be able to assess the cause and extent of the problem and advise whether it can be put right. (See page 115 for choosing a qualified surveyor). If the surveyor advises you that the property can be repaired see chapter 4 for details of your right to repair and financial help with the costs.

If the advice is that the property cannot be repaired and you face the loss of your home, it might be possible to get compensation for the cost of reconstruction or of buying another home depending upon the individual circumstances.

If your home has been built within the past 10 years a National House Building Certificate should still be in force for the property. This provides some protection if there are structural defects as a result of the building or design work. You could contact the NHBC for help and advice. Their address is on page 128.

If your home was built or converted after 1st January 1974, those responsible for constructing it were under a duty imposed by the Defective Premises Act to ensure it was properly built. You can get legal advice from the places mentioned in chapter 9 about claiming compensation for the cost of putting the problem right.

If you have very recently bought your home you will want to know why your surveyor didn't spot the problem and will probably want to take legal advice about claiming compensation from the surveyor (see page 116).

You may be entitled to more straightforward remedies if you were a sitting tenant and bought your home from a local authority or other public landlord (for example, under the Right to Buy). For such owners there is a scheme of repurchase or compensation depending upon when the property was bought and what type of structural problem the home has. The scheme only covers houses and flats built using specific construction systems prescribed by the Government and claims are made to the local council. You can get all the details from the free leaflet *Housing Defects: Help for Private Owners* (Housing Booklet No.18) available from Citizens' Advice Bureaux and other advice centres.

Can my home be taken away by compulsory purchase?

Yes. A surprisingly large number of public authorities and agencies have the power to take away your home by making a compulsory purchase order. Such orders can be made where your property is 'unfit' (see page 62) or the land on which it stands is needed for road widening or for some other public purpose.

If your home is one of several likely to be compulsorily purchased you will probably have some advance warning because the scheme for which the land is needed will have been the subject of considerable local publicity (for example, where it is on the route of a new bypass). Indeed, the fact that a plan or scheme has been adopted for your area might effectively 'blight' your property, making it difficult to sell or reducing its value well before the purchasing authority actually gets round to compulsorily purchasing your home. See page 105 on what to do if your property is affected in this way.

Even if your home is the only one affected you will be given notice of the making of a Compulsory Purchase Order and told of your right to object to the proposed order. Most Compulsory Purchase Orders must be approved by the Secretary of State for the Environment and if there are objections he usually appoints an inspector to conduct a local hearing or inquiry into the proposed order. You have the right to express your point of view and you can be legally represented, but you will have to pay for your own solicitor as no legal aid is available for this type of case (see page 131 on getting legal advice). If you are successful in your objections, the inspector may order your costs to be reimbursed.

If, having received the inspector's report, the Secretary of State confirms the Compulsory Purchase Order there is in practice very little you can do to save your home. You could take legal advice about the possibility of challenging the Secretary of State's decision but more usually you will simply get ready to negotiate adequate compensation for your home and start looking for a new one (see chapter 8, Finding a New Home).

The next step is for the purchasing authority to send you a Notice to Treat. This is the first stage in the price-negotiating process. You have three weeks in which to reply giving notice that you want to claim compensation, but at this stage you don't have to say how much. Next you will need to get professional advice about the amount of your claim. The best person to help on this is a qualified surveyor or valuer (see page 115). You will also need a lawyer to act for you in the sale of the property. Provided you give notice of your claim (as above) in good time, you will be reimbursed for these professional fees by the purchasing authority.

The main item of compensation will be the purchase price for your home and the land on which it stands. In most cases you will receive the market price for your home, that is, the amount at which someone would have been willing to buy (ignoring the CPO) had you been willing to sell. In addition, you will be compensated for the professional costs involved in the sale (see above). Then there will be an added element for 'disturbance', to represent the actual expenses you incur as a result of being forced to move – lawyers and surveyors fees for your new home, removers costs, disconnection and reconnection of appliances.

In addition to these basic categories there are several other types of compensation which can be claimed depending upon the specific circumstances.

If your property is being compulsorily purchased because it is *unfit* the starting point for compensation is the site value of your property (i.e. its value without the buildings on it) and that is what non-resident owners receive. But as an owner-occupier you may be entitled to an *owner-occupier's supplement* to raise the compensation from site value to the true value of your home (see below). Alternatively, you may be eligible for a *well-maintained payment* which is worked out according to the rateable value of your property. If part only of your property is to be taken, you might be compensated for *severance* and if the part which has been acquired will be used in a way which adversely affects what you have left (for example, where your front garden is taken to widen a road) you can claim for *injurious affection.*

Usually, the most important of these is the owner-occupiers supplement. This will probably be the most financially significant because it represents the difference between the cleared site value (for which you will be compensated anyway) and the true market value of your home. to qualify you must show that not only were you the occupier when the formal legal steps were taken but also that at that date you met the residential requirements. These can be met by satisfying one of the following conditions:

(a) you had been in occupation for two years *or*

(b) you are one of a sequence of owner-occupiers who have been in occupation for more than two years *or*

(c) you cannot meet either of the first two conditions but you are an owner-occupier who has been in occupation since purchase, and before you bought you made reasonable inquiries to find out whether the property was likely to be compulsorily purchased.

In calculating periods of occupation, gaps of up to one year are ignored if they are caused by changes in your place of employment or service in the Forces. Other temporary absences (e.g. in hospital or on holiday) are also ignored as long as you have intended throughout to return home.

Precisely because there are so many different components to the compensation you can obtain, you would be well advised to take advice. First read the leaflets *Land Compensation: Your Rights Explained* (a series of five, free from a Citizens' Advice Bureau or other advice centre) and then instruct a surveyor to act for you (see page 115). If the amount of compensation cannot be agreed, the dispute can be referred to the Lands Tribunal (see page

91) which has power to decide the appropriate amount. You can get Legal Aid to help you meet any lawyers' fees at the Lands Tribunal (see page 132).

You will not be able to defer the takeover of your home just by spinning out the negotiations over compensation. The purchasing authority has powers actually to come on to the property to survey and measure up and can force you to move out on giving appropriate notice.

If you are buying your home on a mortgage and it is compulsorily purchased from you because it is unfit, you may find that, because of the 'site value only' rule (see above), you receive as compensation much less than you borrowed on mortgage. In these circumstances you can apply to the local County court which can rescind or vary the mortgage taking into account all relevant matters.

If your home is affected by the 'planning blight' described on page 102, you can sometimes force the purchasing authority into action. You can compel them to buy your home if you meet three conditions: you have occupied the property for more than six months; your home is earmarked from compulsory purchase; you have tried and failed to sell your home at the proper market price. If these conditions apply you can serve notice on the purchasing authority to force them to buy from you **now** rather than later. They have two months within which to accept or deny your claim. Compensation is negotiated under the rules described above.

Sometimes the value of your home will be reduced well before it officially becomes the subject of planning blight. This might happen for example if your home is on a list of 'potentially unfit dwellings' to be inspected by the local authority some years from now. Any potential purchaser discovering this might not be prepared to take a chance and buy your home. If you are affected by this type of situation and it drags on for an unduly long time, consider complaining to the Local Ombudsman (see page 130) about the effect the local authority's inaction is having on your home.

You can supplement the information I have been able to give here about a compulsory purchase by reading the free Government leaflet *Compulsory Purchase Orders: A Guide to Procedure* which is available from Citizens Advice Bureaux and other advice centres.

Can I lose my home through bankruptcy?
Yes, if you are declared bankrupt all your property, including your home if you own it, passes initially to the official receiver appointed by the court which made the declaration. While you are bankrupt you will not be able to buy or lease another home. The official referee, or a trustee later appointed by your creditors, can sell your home as well as your other assets to raise money to repay your debts.

If you own your home on a long lease it may contain a clause declaring that the lease automatically terminates on bankruptcy. In that situation the property does not pass to the official receiver because the lease (and your rights under it) have ended automatically.

If your home is also your family's home, your family may want to try and persuade the official receiver or trustee in bankruptcy to allow them to carry on living there. See pages 56–7 for what happens in these circumstances

Can I lose my home if my marriage or relationship breaks up?
Yes, even if you are the sole legal owner of your home you may be forced to sell it or transfer it to your spouse in proceedings for divorce or judicial separation (see pages 55–6). Where the relationship is one of cohabitation rather than marriage you are less likely to lose it. For a general outline of what happens to your home on the breakdown

of a marriage or relationship see chapter 3 (Your Home & Your Family).

Can my home be repossessed?

Once you have the freehold or leasehold ownership of your home you have the best sort of security of tenure recognized by housing laws. Except in the rather unusual circumstances described earlier in this chapter you should not be at risk of losing your home.

There are two general exceptions to this rule. First, if you are still paying for your home you are at risk of re-possession if you default on your agreement. This is because your home will usually be the 'security' you put up for the loan. See chapter 2 (Paying for Your Home).

Second, if you own your home on a lease there is always the possibility that you might face possession proceedings if you break the terms of your lease. Chapter 7 describes this way of being at risk of 'forfeiting' your home. If you are at risk of losing a home you are buying under a rental purchase agreement, see pages 38–9.

8: Finding a New Home

When might I be looking for a new home?
You might spend the best part of your life in the home you now own but you may want to, or have to, move on. You will have to leave your present home if you have lost the possibility of staying there in one of the ways described in chapter 7 (Losing Your Home) or if, despite the advice in chapter 2 (Paying For Your Home), you can no longer manage the payments on your mortgage. On the other hand you might want to leave your present home in order to move to something smaller, larger, more expensive, less expensive or to a property for some other reason more suitable to your needs or wishes.

In this chapter I consider some of the options available to you in the way of alternative accommodation and offer some advice about the help in getting that accommodation. My assumption is that you are considering selling your present home or it is being sold for you. The first and most important thing to consider is where you will live after you have sold your present home. So do go on and read the rest of this chapter *before* you take any steps towards selling.

How should I go about selling my present home?
Once you have positively decided to sell, you then have to make some key decisions about:

(a) when would be the best time to put your home on the market,

(b) how much your home is worth,

(c) how you are going to make it attractive to buyers,

(d) how you are going to bring it to the attention of buyers,

(e) who is going to handle the legal side of selling your home.

Most people selling their homes get advice on these matters from local estate agents. These days many of them will provide a valuation of your home free of charge and will visit you at home for the purpose. But obviously they hope that you will place the actual selling of your home in their hands. You could invite two or three different agents to give you valuations and use the opportunity of their visits to find out how much they would charge and what services they offer (for example – how many local branches they have, how often they advertise properties, etc). Most charge a fee related to a percentage of the price at which your home is eventually sold. There is nothing to stop you employing two or more agents to sell your home although often there will be a lower charge if you allow one estate agent the 'sole' right to sell your home. You should always try and use an estate agent who is a member of the National Association of Estate Agents as the Association can be helpful if things go wrong (see page 128).

As an alternative to using estate agents you could advertise your home privately, in a local or national newspaper or just by putting a sign in your garden or window or a notice in the local newsagents shop. In some towns and cities there are now property 'shops' where you pay a fixed fee and details of your property are put up on display.

A further possibility is the solicitor's office! Some solicitors now have combined property centres and legal offices where they both advertise homes for sale and carry out the legal side of selling the homes. You can get a list of such places by writing to the National Association of Solicitors Property Centres.

A final possibility would be to sell your home by auction. You may not get as good a price as you would by selling in the normal way, but auctions sometimes mean you get the money much sooner than you otherwise would. Ask a local auctioneer who is a member of the Incorporated Society of Valuers & Auctioneers (address on page 128) for advice about sales by auction locally.

Don't spend a great deal of time and trouble improving or redecorating your home just in order to make it attractive to buyers. There is no reason to suppose that their tastes in wallpaper, etc. will be the same as yours at all. Even some major improvements like double glazing rarely add more to the value of the home than the cost of doing the work.

For the legal side of selling your home see page 114.

Are there any special rules if my present home is on a lease?

Normally you are as free to sell your house if it is held on a lease as you would be if it were freehold. But you need to check the terms of your lease first to make absolutely sure. The words to look for are 'assign' or 'assignment' because these refer to selling or transferring your lease. If your lease says nothing about assignment, all well and good, you can go ahead and sell it.

If your lease says that you can only assign with your lessor's permission, then the person you are going to sell to will want to be sure that you have permission to do so. The law says that the lessor must not unreasonably withhold permission. If your lessor refuses you permission to sell, you should take legal advice (see page 131). Under a law passed in 1988, your landlord must reply to your request for permission within a reasonable time. If he fails to respond you can take the matter to court but again you will need to take legal advice.

The final and rather unlikely possibility is that your lease simply prohibits any assignment. If you find a clause like that in your lease, take legal advice immediately. You may not want to use the same firm of solicitors that you used when you took on the lease as they might be to blame for having allowed that clause to be included.

Selling your lease may not mean that you permanently rid yourself of all responsibility for your former home. Rather curious legal rules mean that there are still some matters you might be responsible for after the new owners have moved in. Ask the person who is handling the legal side of selling your lease about this (see page 114).

What options are there for alternative accommodation?

Most homeowners move from the property they own to a different one which they buy. But if buying again is not the most attractive or sensible option for you personally, there are several other possibilities:

    (a) buying together with another person or group of people
    (b) buying a flat on a lease,
    (c) renting from a housing association,
    (d) renting from a private landlord,
    (e) renting from a local council,
    (f) living in employer-provided accommodation,
    (g) moving to a community home (such as a residential care or nursing home).

If you are unable to arrange alternative accommodation and you lose your present home, you face the prospect of homelessness. The help available in that situation is described on page 123.

What is best for you depends on your own individual circumstances but in the following pages I offer some general advice.

How do I go about buying an alternative home?

You need to start with some basic decisions about the sort

of area you want to live in, the size of accommodation you are looking for and so on. Some of the larger building societies and estate agents have free leaflets or booklets about buying a home which set out the main things to look out for. One of the best free guides is *Starting Point: A Building Society Guide to House Purchase* available from the Building Societies Association (address on page 128). But for most people who are buying again the most crucial question is: how much can I afford? This is obviously all the more critical if the reason for moving is because of financial difficulties in your present home.

There are two elements to working out how much you can afford to spend on your new home: first, how much you will realize from the sale of your present home and, second, how much on top of that you will need to borrow. You can work out how much you will realize from your present home as follows:

(a) Estimate what you will sell your home for (by getting valuations from estate agents as described on page 109).

(b) Deduct what it will cost to repay any current mortgages or loans secured on the property (you will need to ask your lenders for 'redemption figures' for each of your loans).

(c) Deduct what it is going to cost you to sell (by getting estimates of estate agents' fees and of solicitors' charges).

That will give you a figure for the balance or 'capital' you will realize from selling your home. But that is not the same as what you will have available to spend. There will be other deductions: the costs of removals, disconnections and reconnections, legal fees on the new purchase and, of course, the costs of any additional furnishings or essential repairs needed in your new home. It is only the balance left as a capital sum after those deductions that you will really have free to spend.

(If you are receiving a social security benefit for which savings are relevant (such as income support, see page 29) don't worry about the effect of this 'capital' figure. It will be ignored for 6 months or longer to give you time to buy your new home.)

If you think the capital realized will not give you enough to buy a new home outright you will have to borrow to make up the difference. If you have had a satisfactory mortgage before and you were happy with the service provided by your lender, you could go back to them to arrange a new home loan. Otherwise, shop around. There are many building societies, banks and lending institutions willing to lend money on mortgages. They are generally the cheapest types of lender and are in competition with one another so you should certainly shop around for the 'best buy' in terms of quality of service and help available. Try and steer clear of finance companies and other lenders who generally charge higher rates of interest. The lending institutions will want to know: what gross income you (and any partner) have, how much capital you will realize from selling your present home, how much you want to borrow and the likelihood of your being able to make the repayments.

If you are selling because of problems with your previous homeloan you may find it more difficult to get a new mortgage arrangement but you should certainly try your original lender and two or three different banks and building societies. Be ready to explain to them why it is you will now be able to manage (perhaps because you are buying a cheaper property or recent financial difficulties have been resolved). Your local council (the District or Borough Council) has the power to grant mortgages or could alternatively act as guarantor to help you get a mortgage with another lender. You could make inquiries with the Mortgage Department or Housing Officer at your local council. You could also ask your local councillor to help with your application.

Once you have found a lender willing to offer you a mortgage, you need to consider what type of mortgage will be best for you. You may already have had experience with one type of mortgage. All the different varieties are explained on pages 19–21. It's a good idea to ask your potential lender to work out for you what the monthly repayments would be for you under each of the different types of mortgage before you make your choice.

Once you have your financial position clear or a new mortgage agreed in principle, you can set off hunting for your new home.

If you are looking for sheltered accommodation (that is the sort of accommodation where a personal service – such as a resident warden facility – is provided for the benefit of older or disabled occupiers) you may find it worthwhile to obtain the *Buyers Guide to Sheltered Housing*, from Age Concern (address on page 67).

If you are buying a flat, you might find the publication *Buying a Flat?* useful. It is produced jointly by the Law Society and the Royal Institution of Chartered Surveyors (address on page 127).

Will I need a solicitor to handle the sale of my current home and the purchase of a new one?

Most people use solicitors to handle the legal side of buying and selling their homes. In recent years the effect of advertising and greater competition has forced some solicitors to reduce the charge they make for this type of work and by 'shopping around' it should be possible to find a solicitor willing to do the legal work at a reasonable rate (but make sure you are being quoted a firm price including all the extras such as VAT and the various official payments or 'disbursements' the solicitor will need to make).

As an alternative you could use a licensed conveyancer. This person will have received professional training in handling the legal side of buying and selling homes. They might also charge less than a solicitor. You can get a list of names and addresses of local conveyancers from the National Association of Conveyancers, 2–4 Chichester Rents, Chancery Lane, London WC2.

Another possibility would be to do the legal work yourself. There are several books available which explain the steps in detail. These include *Which? The Legal Side of Buying a House* from the Consumers Association, *D-I-Y Conveyancing* (Prism Press, 1987) and *The D-I-Y Conveyancing Kit* (Michael Joseph, 1989).

As a general guide you could try *Buying and Selling Your Home (A Teach Yourself Guide)* Hodder & Stoughton 1980.

Should I have a survey done on the home I want to buy?

Definitely. Your lender will have their own survey done to see whether the house or flat is worth the money being loaned on it (a survey you usually have to pay for as part of the lender's costs). But you will want a very different survey done for yourself because you are going to live in the property and need to know at the outset what condition it is in and what work it might need. It may seem odd paying hundreds of pounds for a survey of a house you are not sure you want to buy, but a full structural survey can reveal defects that would cost thousands of pounds to put right and could save you considerable time and effort. You might find you can reduce the costs of a full structural survey by using the same surveyor as your lender is using for the valuation survey. Ask your lender which surveyor they use or suggest to them a surveyor you are going to use.

Most good surveyors are members of the Royal Institution of Chartered Surveyors so when choosing one to employ look out for the letters RICS or FRICS, or choose a valuer who is a member of the Incorporated Society of Valuers & Auctioneers. The Royal Institution (address on page 127) can supply a list of their members working in your area and they publish two useful free leaflets *What is a Building Survey?* and *Valuations & Surveys* which are available on request.

Normally the survey report (whether commissioned by your lender or by you) will be accurate and correctly reflect the state and value of the property. Most surveyors and valuers insure against the possibility of making mistakes or overlooking particular problems. Indeed, a recent court case has established that you have the right to sue the surveyor if a negligently prepared report causes you to buy a home which later turns out to be defective or require substantial repair. This applies whether the survey you relied upon was the one commissioned by your lender or the one you commissioned. Your right to sue cannot be barred by a disclaimer notice such as 'this report is issued without responsibility for its accuracy'. If you feel you were let down by your surveyor take legal advice (page 131).

When should I take out insurance on the new home?

As soon as you exchange contracts for your new home. This is the moment when you become legally committed to buying the house or flat (it will be some days or weeks before everything is legally completed and you can move in). You need to take out insurance at that stage because if the house or flat burned down you could be legally obliged to carry on and pay the agreed price for a burned-out shell. If you are taking out a mortgage for a new home your lender will probably arrange this insurance but you need to check.

Don't just switch your present home insurance to covering the home you want to buy as this will leave your present home unprotected. It is better to take out a new policy and then, when you have moved, cash in the old one with a refund for any unexpired period.

What is a bridging loan?

This is a straightforward temporary loan for which you pledge your new home as security. You might need a bridging loan to complete the purchase of a home you want to buy for a very short period before your new permanent mortgage comes through or the cash becomes available from the sale of your old home.

If possible you should avoid bridging loans as they can be charged at very high rates of interest and if not repaid can be enforced by making you sell your new home. You should never take out such a loan unless you are absolutely sure that the permanent funds you need will definitely be available in the very near future.

Are there any special rules if the home I want to buy is a flat?

Most flats in this country are sold on leases. Owning on a lease is a special type of ownership and is very different to what you may have experienced if you were previously the owner of a freehold house. An explanation of the difference between freehold and leasehold is given on pages 3–5. There is information about freehold flats on page 11 and leasehold houses on pages 4–5.

In general the legal side of buying a flat can be slightly more complex than simply buying a freehold house. You need especially to consider such matters as ground rents (see pages 42–3) and service charges (see pages 43–5). It is usually well worth having a solicitor to check over the lease of the flat you want to buy.

If you are definitely going ahead with buying a flat, there is a book you may find very useful called *Owning Your Flat* (£2.50 from SHAC, 189a Old Brompton Road, London SW5 0AR).

How would I go about buying with others rather than on my own?

Buying with others might have advantages for you if you are prepared to consider sharing and would want to buy a more substantial property than you could afford on your own.

You will find much useful information about this option in the handbook *Buying Your Home with Other People* by Dave Treanor (available from Shelter Publications, 88 Old Street, London E1V 9HU for £5.95).

Could I partly buy and partly rent my new home?

Yes. This is called *shared ownership* and there is a description of how it works on page 13.

If you are interested in shared ownership, you will probably find that the organizations most likely to share the ownership of property with you are local councils and housing associations.

A good place to start finding out more is the free leaflet *Shared Ownership: How to Become a Home-Owner in Stages* (Housing Booklet No.15) which you can get from your local consumer advice centre or Citizens' Advice Bureau.

Most shared ownership schemes are geared towards first-time buyers but there is no reason for not applying if you are moving to a new home.

Can a housing association help me with accommodation?

A housing association might be able to help you in one of three ways. They might be prepared to buy your present home from you but allow you to carry on living there as their tenant. Alternatively, they could buy your home on the basis that they will rehouse you as a tenant in one of their other properties. Finally, if you sell your present home privately they might be prepared to offer you one of their normal tenancies.

Housing association tenancies are reasonably attractive as most associations are responsible landlords and their tenancy conditions offer reasonably good security. Most of the property they have is rented out unfurnished so you will be able to make use of the fittings and furnishings from your current home. Recent changes to housing laws, however, now mean that their rents are becoming more like those charged by private landlords (although if you are on a low or modest income you can get financial help with the rent by claiming housing benefit from your local council). If the housing association is going to buy your home they may not pay as much for it as you could get if you sold it yourself but on the other hand they are going to offer to rehouse you permanently so it is a possibility you might want to pursue.

The Housing Department of your local council should have a list of the housing associations operating in the area where you want to live. Alternatively you could contact the National Federation of Housing Associations at 175 Gray's Inn Rd, London WC1X 8UP, to see if they can give you details of housing associations offering the type of accommodation more particularly suited to your needs. The Housing Corporation (which has regional offices responsible for the funding and supervision of local housing associations) may be able to help. Their head office is at 149 Tottenham Court Rd, London W1P 0BN (01 387 9466). A local advice centre or Citizens' Advice Bureau might also be able to help with names and addresses. Many housing associations have very long waiting lists for their housing and others will give priority to people with more urgent housing needs than your own but there is no harm to be done by approaching the associations and a lot to be gained.

Should I consider renting from a private landlord?

This is unlikely to be an attractive option if you have had your own home for some time. Reasonably priced unfurnished accommodation (which you will need for the possessions and furnishings moved from your current home) is very hard indeed to come by. Also, recent changes to the law mean that it will not be possible for you to find a home with as much security as was available under the old Rent Acts.

If you are offered the possibility of accommodation that seems to suit, do consider the terms of the arrangement offered very carefully. Is there a premium to be paid? Will there be a deposit? Is the rent payable in advance? What are the other terms of the agreement? – and so on. The best idea is to take advice **before** entering into an agreement. If your local council has a housing aid centre, approach them for advice. If not, try a local advice centre such as a citizens' advice bureau.

For a general explanation of your rights if you rent private accommodation see the *Private Tenants Handbook* available in this series.

If you are on a low or modest income you can get financial help with the rent charged by applying for housing benefit from the local District or Borough Council.

How would I go about getting a council house or flat when I leave my present home?

There are still some parts of the country where it is possible simply to ask for a council house or flat and be allocated one straight away. However, it is much more likely that council homes are in high demand in the area where you want to live and there is a waiting list for the allocation of accommodation.

You should put your name on the waiting list for the area you want to live in as soon as the possibility arises of your giving up your present home. Some councils will say, 'We don't register homeowners on the list', but this is wrong. Your local housing advice or other advice centre will be able to help if this happens to you.

Once you are on the list you will have to wait until accommodation becomes available. In some areas the list operates in date order. In others the allocations are made according to the 'priority' you have as a result of your housing needs. If you are presently satisfactorily housed you will get very little priority. Check how the scheme works in your area. Every council has to publish a summary of the rules under which it allocates it homes, so ask for a copy of the leaflet or handbook which does this at the local Housing Department office.

Most councils let their properties unfurnished and on secure tenancies which offer a very reasonable degree of security. By law the council can only charge a 'reasonable' rent for its flats and houses.

There is a great deal more information about being a council tenant in the *Public Tenants Handbook* also available in this series.

If you were previously a council tenant and bought your present home from the council they may be prepared to buy it back from you while allowing you to stay on as their tenant. Ask about this possibility at your local Housing Department Office.

If you feel that the council is not dealing with your case properly ask to see your local councillor and get him or her to look into the matter. If you are still not satisfied you could complain to the local ombudsman (see page 129–30).

How do I go about getting a place in a retirement, residential care or nursing home when I sell my present home?
If you are considering living in this type of accommod-

ation there are basically three choices: a privately run home, a home run by a voluntary organization (sometimes a charity or religious order) or a council owned home.

All three have some connection with the Social Services Department of the County or Regional Council for the area where you want to live. This is because most privately run homes have to be registered with (and are inspected by) social service officials. As a result, the obvious place to start looking for a suitable home is at the offices of your local Social Services Department. They should be able to provide you with a list of all the private and voluntary homes in the area as well as help you with details of their own residential homes. Age Concern (address on page 67) have a free guide called *Choosing an Old People's Home* which you may find useful. Taking a place in one of these homes is a very important step. You will be selling or passing on your own home, probably selling much of your furniture and possessions and entering into a wholly new financial arrangement for this sort of accommodation. It is, therefore, well worth taking advice before you move. The social services staff in particular would be worth talking to as they may be able to arrange the care and support you are seeking in your own home rather than your needing to move. You could also take some independent advice about the financial side because even the council homes can be expensive. Finally, why not try out living in the home of your choice for a 'trial period' of a few weeks before you part with your present home?

Private and voluntary homes usually make a weekly or monthly charge and can be very expensive indeed. You will not find anything for less than £100 per week. If you are on a low or modest income you might be able to get financial help with the costs by claiming the benefit income support (how to do this is explained on page 29).

122

Ask at your nearest DSS office for the relevant free leaflet which has all the details. In working out what benefit you are entitled to, the DSS will not take into account the value of your former home while you are selling it, although once you have sold it the proceeds will be counted as savings available to you. You can't avoid this rule just by giving your home away or passing over the proceeds to your friends or relatives.

If you are thinking about leaving your present home because it no longer suits your needs and you are a disabled person, you might find the *Disabled Persons Handbook* (available in this series) worth reading before you make any final decisions.

What if I am going to lose my present home and cannot arrange another permanent home to move to?

Very starkly, you face the possibility of homelessness. Fortunately, people faced with homelessness have a legal right to help from the local housing authority. The help available ranges from just advice about finding another home to a duty to arrange permanent accommodation for you. It all depends on your own personal circumstances and why you become homeless. You can find out what the local authority will provide for you by making an application to the Homelessness Officer or Homeless Persons Unit of the council in the area where you want to iv You can make the application while you are still a l owner. The staff will look into your circumstances give you a written decision about what help you entitled to.

Even while you still have your house or flat, the cou could accept you as homeless if they decide it is 'n reasonable' for you to continue in occupation. This might be because there is something wrong with your property, or you are very overcrowded or perhaps because you can no longer afford your home and face repossession by your mortgage lender. One judge has said that it would not be reasonable for an owner-occupier to continue in occupation if he or she could only meet their housing costs by going without other basic necessities such as food, clothing or fuel. If you are accepted as homeless in this way, that means that the council can deal with your application long before you are literally 'roofless'.

If your home is already being repossessed and you are within 28 days of a possession order expiring, the council must accept you as threatened with homelessness. If you didn't deliberately bring this situation about yourself and you are in a priority group (for example because you are elderly or have children) the council must make sure that you continue to have some housing. It can do this either by preventing the eviction from your present home (for example by having your mortgage transferred to the council or by underwriting your present home loan) or by providing you with alternative accommodation to move to.

There are lots of variations of the type of help you can expect and what the local council are obliged to provide. All the details are set out in the *Homeless Persons Handbook* available in this series from libraries or bookshops.

If you are not satisfied with the way the council responds to your application, take the matter up with your local councillor. If still not satisfied, take advice from a local Citizens' Advice Bureau or other advice centre.

What if I am offered accommodation by my new employer?

If you want to take the job and accommodation that is offered with it (whether rent free or otherwise), all well and good. But selling your own home in order to do so raises a number of important issues.

First you should consider whether it might not be best

to keep your home while you are away. That way you can return to it when you retire or leave your new job. You could let your house to tenants while you are away and be reasonably sure that when you need your home back again you will be able to get possession (see page 75).

Next, you need to consider carefully the terms on which the employer is offering you accommodation. If the accommodation is offered so that you will be able to perform your job better by being close at hand (or it is a condition of your employment that you occupy the accommodation and it is manifestly more convenient to your job requirements that you live there), you will be treated by the law as a 'service occupier'. This means you have very limited rights to stay in the property once your employer asks you to leave. If you have sold your former home you will face the very real prospect of homelessness.

Only slightly better security is available if your employer provides you with accommodation because you are an employee (even though you don't strictly need to be in the employer's accommodation in order to perform your job better), whether you pay for the house or flat or get it rent free. The law will treat you as a service tenant with a proper tenancy, but there are lots of circumstances in which you will get less protection or less security in your home than other tenants, just because your home is provided by your employer. The rules are rather different if you are working in agriculture and your employer provides accommodation.

For the best information on the rights you would have in employer-provided accommodation see the *Tied Accommodation Handbook* available in this series.

9: Making Complaints and Getting Advice

Why should I make a complaint?
As a homeowner you will have reason from time to time to use the services of other people or organizations – from surveyors to solicitors and from contractors to councils. On most occasions you will be provided with a good standard of service at a reasonable price. This chapter is written to help you deal with those situations in which you may not have received reasonable service or you have been overcharged.

In Britain we have for too long been reluctant to press our complaints and, where appropriate, claim compensation. This attitude has allowed poor quality services to persist. In recent years, responsible organizations have established facilities for the handling of customer and consumer complaints in order to eliminate from the system those providers of slipshod or inadequate services. In some cases, if the complaint is upheld, compensation is payable.

For a homeowner dissatisfied with the service he or she has received, making a complaint not only helps to prevent others suffering from the same poor quality service but may also provide the possibility of redress and financial compensation.

What is the best way to make a complaint?
A good way to start is to make a personal approach to the individual or organization responsible for the difficulty. If they are unresponsive, put your complaint in writing to the firm or organization for which they work. Address your letter to the Manager or Senior Officer and keep a copy. Always try and make your complaint promptly. It

will be much easier to investigate and follow up if you act swiftly.

Some large organizations and companies have their own in-house complaints procedures (most building societies and local authorities do). Make inquiries at the nearest branch or office of the organization and get details of the complaints process.

If there is no internal complaints procedure or it does not provide satisfaction, you will have to pursue your complaint to the independent authorities. Making such a complaint will usually cost you no more than the time and . effort of writing out (and making a copy of) your grievance.

As a homeowner you are very likely at some time to use the following service providers. In relation to each of them I give details of the relevant complaints authority.

Solicitors

Every solicitor is a member of a professional organization called the Law Society. It can ultimately expel members for malpractice. Complaints are investigated in the first instance by the Solicitors' Complaints Bureau which has a leaflet setting out how to complain about a solicitor. The Law Society is at 113 Chancery Lane, London WC2A 1PL (01 242 1222) and the Solicitors' Complaints Bureau is at Portland House, Storey Place, London SW1 (01 834 2288).

Surveyors

Most good surveyors are members of the Royal Institution of Chartered Surveyors. It will investigate complaints about its members. Its address is 12 Great George St., London SW1P 3AD (01 222 7000).

Valuers

Most reputable valuers are members of the Incorporated

Society of Valuers and Auctioneers. Complaints about one of its members can be sent to the ISVA at 3 Cadogan Gate, London SW1 0AS (01 235 2282).

Estate agents

Estate agents may work independently or as part of a large national or regional group. If you are not satisfied with the services of one of the local branches of a group or chain, try pursuing your complaint with their head office. Many estate agents are members of the National Estate Agents Association. If you are dissatisfied with the service you have received from a member write to them at Arbon House, 21 Jury St., Warwick CV34 4EH (0926 496800).

Building Societies

A complaint unresolved at local branch level can be referred to the society's head office. If you are still not satisfied, you could complain to the Building Societies Association at 3 Savile Row, London W1X 1AF (01 436 0695). There is also now a building society ombudsman to look into complaints. Write for a leaflet and complaint form to the Office of the Building Societies Ombudsman, 35-37 Grosvenor Gardens, London SW1X 7AW (01 961 0044).

Builders

If you have bought your home from a builder or your home was constructed not long before you became the owner, any difficulty you have may be covered by the building certificate for the property guaranteed by the National House Building Council. You can write to them at 58 Portland Place, London W1N 4BU (01 580 9381).

If the builder is a member of one of the large builders' associations, you could write to the association for help.

The Federation of Master Builders, for example, is at 33 John St., London WC1N 2BB (01 242 7583).

Insurance companies

The starting point for your complaint should be a letter to the regional or head office of the company. If this produces no satisfaction, consider complaining to the Association of British Insurers (of which the company is probably a member) at Aldermary House, Queen Street, London EC4N 1TT. If your complaint is about a specific insurance claim ask for a complaint form or explanatory leaflet from the Insurance Ombudsman, 31 Southampton Row, London WC1B 5HJ.

Contractors

If you have followed the advice on pages 67–69 about using the services of contractors, you will have a written contract on which you can rely for compensation if services are not satisfactory. If you can't get the work finished or it is inadequate, take advice about enforcing your agreement (see pages 130–131).

If you employed a contractor who is or was a member of one of the professional associations, try sending your complaint to the association. Among the larger ones are: Institution of Electrical Engineers, Savoy Place, London WC2 (01 240 1871) and Heating & Ventilation Contractors Association, 24 Palace Court, London W2 4JG.

Local Councils

If you have been let down by the services of a local council or are disappointed by the decision of a council, a good place to start with your complaint is with the local councillor for your area. Your local library or town hall can give you the name, address and sometimes telephone number of your local ward councillor (either for a County or District Council).

If you are still dissatisfied after seeing the councillor, consider making a complaint to the Commissioner for Local Administration (the local ombudsman). Write to the Commission at 21 Queen Anne's Gate, London SW1H 9BU (01 222 5622) for a free explanatory booklet and complaint form. If your complaint relates to a council in Wales write to the Commissioner for Wales, Derwen House, Court Road, Bridgend, Mid-Glamorgan CF31 1BN (0656 61325).

Government Departments

If you feel you have received poor service from a Government Department (like the Land Registry (page 14) or Department of Social Security (page 29)) write to your local Member of Parliament or arrange to meet him or her. Your local library or town hall can give you the MPs name and correspondence address. The MP may even have a surgery which you could visit.

If the MP cannot help, or the outcome is unsatisfactory, ask the MP to refer your case to the Parliamentary Commissioner for Administration (the Ombudsman) for an investigation.

Where can I get general advice?

In many areas of the country you will find there is a local advice centre offering a free general advice service. Citizens' Advice Bureaux have the largest network (over 900 nationwide). They deal with all sorts of housing and other matters and can help direct you for more specialist or legal advice to other organizations or solicitors.

You can find your nearest Citizens' Advice Bureau from the telephone directory where they are listed under 'C'. Alternatively ring the National Association of Citizens' Advice Bureaux (01 833 2181) for the local addresses and telephone numbers.

There are many other local and independent advice centres. Your local library will have details of the ones operating in your area. The Federation of Independent Advice Centres (01 274 1839) may also have a member organization in your area.

What about specialist advice on housing?

There are quite a few housing aid and housing advice centres. Some are run by local councils and others operate independently. Ask at your local library or town hall for the details of the nearest housing advice centre, or call the national housing charity Shelter at 88 Old St., London EC1 (01 253 0202) and ask if there is a housing aid centre they know of in your area.

If you are in or around London, the organization SHAC can often help at their London Housing Aid Centre, 189a Old Brompton Road, London SW5 0AR (01 373 7276).

If you want advice about financial aspects of running your home (help with mortgage payments for example) ring or write for expert advice to Housing Debtline at The Birmingham Settlement, 318 Summer Road, Birmingham B19 3RL (021 359 8501).

How do I go about getting legal advice?

You might think the most obvious starting point would be to approach a solicitor. However, if you have not used a solicitor before or you need to be directed to one specialising in a particular type of work, approach a general advice centre first (see page 130). They may be able to direct you to a specialist or advise you about how solicitors charges operate and how the legal aid scheme works (see below). Alternatively there may be a Law Centre or Legal Advice Centre serving your area. You could telephone the National Law Centres Federation (01 387 8570) to find out.

When you do see a solicitor, remember that he or she will need to be paid for his or her services. It is worth getting clear at the outset just how much the advice is going to cost. Some solicitors offer a 'fixed fee interview' scheme under which you pay a small flat fee for up to 30 minutes of advice. Ask about that when you make your appointment to see the solicitor. If you cannot easily manage lawyers' fees you may qualify for legal aid (see below).

The *Lawyer/Client Handbook* (available in this series) deals with making the most of your employment of a solicitor.

What is legal aid?

Legal aid is a national scheme run by the Legal Aid Board. It uses Government money to pay lawyers' fees for those on low or modest incomes who would not otherwise be able to afford the costs of legal advice or representation. The lower your financial resources the more likely you are to get your legal help free or at reduced cost. You can get a free explanatory leaflet about how the scheme works by writing to the Legal Aid Board at Newspaper House, 8-16 Great New Street, London EC4A 3BN 01 353 7411).

You should ask your solicitor about legal aid the first time you meet him. He will advise you on whether you are likely to be entitled. The Legal Aid Board will meet the costs (in whole or in part) of up to two hour's work as initial help from a lawyer under the Advice & Assistant part of the Scheme. Your solicitor works out on the spot how much free help you qualify for. If your case has to go to court the solicitor will send off an application for full legal aid to the Board. The Board may ask you to pay towards the costs and if you win your case it will recoup what it spends on your behalf from any funds or property you recover or keep.